A Doctrine
Of
Creative Education

*

Traumear

Paperback ISBN 978-0-244-14402-9

*

www.traumear.com

★

This is a comprehensive work, setting forth in detail how creative education can operate. Described and observed in practice are the skills of the educator of both children and adults. Emphasis is placed on human nature as inwardly original and outwardly communicable, and on the ability of the teacher to deal with the pupils' disabilities and inabilities as initially transferred to himself. Comparison is drawn with standard and artistic education.

★

A Doctrine of Creative Education

Human nature is something we need to be sure about. We experience that in ourselves, this pressing need to know who we are and what we amount to. Some of us existed for long enough before it occurred to us that what was bothering us was our insecurity with respect to why we exist, just here and now rather than elsewhere at some other time. The question: Why was I born? usually means: Why here and now?

A *certain insecurity* – the expression seems to contain a contradiction. Logic dictates we can either be certain or insecure, not both. But then logic belongs to the head, while that certain insecurity springs from closer to the centre of our human being, namely the heart, seat of faith, motor of will and emotion. Think of the human breast as the source and resource of love and soon you cease to wonder why here first insecurity should be felt and resented. Is anyone ever too young to feel it? Never too young, only perhaps to identify it, to name it, to talk about it; to say: „This insecurity is upon me; I remember it from last time." It becomes that *certain* insecurity only then, when time and repetition have worn a groove for it in our sensibilities. Only then do we behave like the man who had become attached to his pain because no other sensation had been left him. We get used to *our* insecurity, become cynical or sarcastic with respect to it, haughty in the face of it, prone to cowardice or self-justification.

The only thing certain about it is its frequent resurrection, to which we give a variety of names, to comfort ourselves or to keep it at a distance. We speak about it *breaking out*, and then afterwards we pretend nothing happened. We malinger in it and gradually the world takes on a questionable aspect, since more and more we paint our environment in the colours of it, drab or shrill, monotonous or exaggerated.

That certain insecurity is not laid with us into our cradle, however. We are not born with it. It makes a difference to us, if we think it is, though it is not. No one is born insecure. All the same, with the light of day it begins for us. Let no one hinder those who surround the newly born babe with all the care and attention in the world, especially if the natural mother is not able.

What we are born with is a capacity for *care*. No one can deny that. To think more of another than of myself, that is care. Who is it knows really how to care – and does it – often – even sometimes? Is it a capacity for care, or an ability to care we are born with? Some with one, and some with the other?

2

As soon as we care, our insecurity is gone. We can speculate why this should be so. Evidently there is a correlation between that existential insecurity and what we do when we care. It may take years, even decades, before we finally come around to making a point of caring, even when we do *not* feel that insecurity. But initially the most difficult of all things in the world is to turn our own insecurity, whenever we experience it and for whatever reason we suppose we experience it, into care. Because that is the reason for the insecurity: a habit of care.

We cannot be made to care, by a drive or by circumstances. An intentional and conscious act is required. And yet we would never learn how to care if we did not first experience – not a careless existence, because that can seem ever so fine for a time – but real and absolute insecurity, which is, after all, a manifest need for care and for caring. We would never know what a precious thing it is to care if we did not first experience what a horrible thing it is not to care. And that is what this awful insecurity amounts to, namely an uncaring existence.

Of course we use this word *care* in so many ways. "I don't care for that sort of pudding." "I don't care any more what happens to me." We speak of a careworn person. But the care we mean here, in relation to that *fundamental* insecurity – perhaps we should call it a radical insecurity – is the care for another or for others more than for ourselves.

That complicates matters. One might prefer simply to equate care with a liking for something or for others, or with a taking care of, in the sense of supporting another's survival. But that would be avoiding the main issue. What we mean is a proper and fitting response to the type of insecurity that is not a type of it at all but the dreaded thing itself. Such insecurity, as we implied above, can be difficult to countenance. On some occasions it seethes within us like an acid, so that the whole world shuns us, and little wonder. Who wants to be reminded of his basic insecurity? And yet, who will care to care – who can even learn to care – except from within such an experience of insecurity?

The point is that the insecurity springs up from our individuality and from it alone – while the care is personal. A great gulf can occur, something like a yawning abyss, between us as individuals and us as persons, so that the connection between the two bears all the marks of impossibility and despair.

3

If there is one thing that we human beings must learn, it is to care. We could say love instead of care, but we want to emphasize the need to make room in ourselves for that other individuality. Our own individuality tends to fill us out to the brim until nothing is left for anyone else to relate to. One individual is death to the other. From within our individuality we see nothing but replicas of ourselves, and these remain firmly closed to us.

Another reason why we say care instead of love is our interest in education, specifically, which has to do with learning and teaching, both of which relate intimately to care. If

3

you would teach me without caring for me you will fail. If I would learn something without care I will fail.

The road from one individuality to another is fraught with pitfalls, and these pitfalls vary, from culture to culture and from age to age. It is up to us to deal specifically with those of our own culture and our own age. We live here and now for the purpose of doing good here and now.

4

We are radically insecure to the extent that we do not care. But our insecurity is not always plain and obvious to us, as experience, such as a feeling of panic or a thought of despair or a will to destroy. When these are upon us we can say: Yes, I am radically insecure. But actually we have been insecure for some time, without knowing. Something triggered the experience where previously we were unaware of it but all the same insecure. Of course we are free at any time to test ourselves for such hidden insecurity, for example by turning out gaze inward and contemplating our human nature. If we are readily able to do that, for a time that allows us to be truthfully persuaded that this is indeed what we are doing, then we have no such insecurity to worry about, and nothing to gain by further contemplation of our human nature. If, however, this suggestion to contemplate our human nature sounds absurd, then there is cause for concern. Our human nature should always be open and freely accessible to me. Our human nature comprises how we were born and what we were born with. If that has disappeared from our gaze we are lost. To be lost means the same as to be radically insecure. How fortunate, therefore, to have such a test at our disposal!

5

My human nature is something I can contemplate. My reason for doing so is the removal of all radical insecurity. When I set out to contemplate my human nature, hindrances prevent me. I make it my task to overcome these hindrances.

They are themselves my own human nature, but falsified aspects and extensions of it. These hindrances let me know that my nature is to that extent and to that degree false. My contemplation is a valuable tool, because it highlights these falsifications of my nature for me, at a time I have myself chosen. If I let fate and circumstances do the highlighting for me, it becomes a predicament or a disaster, which is no guarantee of opened eyes or subsequent progress.

Before we set out on the main part or our doctrine it would be advisable to learn such verification of our human nature via contemplation of it, otherwise much of what will be said will be misunderstood. It would make little sense to speak of human nature as something that responds to education if our own human nature were not intact. Such a book as this is not to appeal to many, but to a few. Only a few actually desire to become aware of their radical insecurity, because they know, perhaps by creative imagination, perhaps by hopeful intelligence, how much can be achieved in terms of a fundamentally secure human nature. Good spirit cannot touch a false nature.

So as I set out to contemplate my human nature, I may be hindered by the suspicion, sarcastically or cynically reinforced, that no such thing exists. As I persevere, assuming that it does exist but that I cannot access it, I may be hindered by fatigue or high spirits. These are to put me off and I must simply refuse to be put off. I have help. I draw strength from the certainty I have now that my human nature exists, which certainty I deduce from the event of the fatigue or the high spirits. Again I persevere. I can never again now doubt that my human nature exists, since I have had, and no doubt will again have, evidence of it. This certainty is secure. I intend to put it into practice by persevering with contemplation of my human nature in the face of high spirits or fatigue.

Remarkable that high spirits should constitute a hindrance. Correct all the same.

Do I contemplate the high spirits or the fatigue? No, because those are the hindrances. If I did, I would soon run aground. Do I contemplate my human nature independently or somehow separately from these? No, because these hindrances to contemplation are after all human nature all the same, though falsified. So the correct approach is that I contemplate my human nature inclusive of these hindrances.

The high spirits would tend to draw me away from my intention, to something more attractive, so I will persevere in spite of that. The fatigue would tend to get me bogged down, to concentrate on the hindrance rather than on my goal.

At the same time I remain alert for other hindrances. The back-and-forth between fatigue and high spirits might, for example, give way to a degree of self-appreciation, where I begin to rely on an automatic feed-back, with which I am then supplied too, richly; anything to put me off the track. It would be fine now if I were in the possession of some criteria which would allow me to recognize my nature and to recognize an all too natural response to my contemplation – that is all the same false. What I called 'automatic feed-back' can only be identified in relation to, or rather in reference to, my contemplation itself, because it simply turns contemplation off, so that a thoughtless, unfeeling and unintentional activity takes over.

The contemplation we mean is active. Something goes on, something is done and there is an effect. The purpose of it is the discovery and revelation of my true human nature. When this contemplation comes to its end, therefore, a true human natural activity takes over which can be seen as my previous contemplation plus a response to it. The whole of it is then called real action. It is important that we do not mistake the previously encountered 'automatic feed-back' for real action. So we do well to make certain that our contemplation is not displaced, by something that is often called super- this or that, such as supernatural, superhuman. We continue with contemplation until it is completed and perfected. Then we are really acting. That perfected contemplation is real action. It lets us know that there is more to our human nature than we can cause. There is more than we can manipulate, control or force.

There is that about our human nature which is willing to cause. We encounter it as the end and goal of our contemplation. Certain attributes of it, such as peace, joy and rest, render it unmistakable.

We were born with this capacity for peace, joy and rest; we do not first have to earn or deserve it. The cares and woes that plague us can all be seen as falsifications of our nature. On the other hand, there are the cares and woes of those we care for and love, and we take these cares and woes upon ourselves, so that those we love and we ourselves might freely live.

If I care enough for you to take your care upon me, I truly care for you.

This is true care, that swallows the cares of others.

7

When first we make contact with our human nature, after having succumbed to falsification, there is great rejoicing. The most human natural impulse then is to broadcast the good news. This impulse is tempered and made perfect by way of discipline, discernment and discrimination. These three add up to what we mean by *temperament*. In the absence of this, dissipation sets in, so that what we gain with one hand is wasted with the other. The cultivation of temperament is therefore of crucial importance.

8

A thorough understanding of temperament will allow us more insight into what we can do for one another in terms of teaching and learning.

Let us begin by asking ourselves how often we look outside ourselves for guidance or guidelines when we set out to do something. If I make a table, I look outside for measurements, dimensions, shape or purpose, that sort of thing, but only if I earn my money at table-making and am financially motivated. It is immaterial to me what the table looks like, how good a table it is, whether it will fall down after a week if someone commits the foolishness of setting a plate on it. I intend to use this expression 'outside' myself to indicate an aspect of irresponsible behaviour. Here am I: that is then my essential interest, and everything that I make use of out there to serve that interest I consider to be outside myself. When you come along, I make sure you stay outside, so that I can make you too serve my advantage. Of course while I am lost in this kind of a backwater of existence, I do not myself use the expression 'outside myself' to mean anything at all, but anyone who is to any degree in contact with reality might readily reflect on my foolishness and observe that I am guided from outside myself.

So that is what we mean right now ourselves, by guidance from outside. It should at all costs be avoided, naturally, and when we think about what to do instead, we might be told by someone – to look inside ourselves instead.

Now inside myself I hear voices, I see signs pointing this way and that way, while certain hardened opinions that were, by the way, forced into me at one time from 'outside', behave quite dictatorially 'inside' me now. Attitudes towards the world, towards table etiquette, towards god and creation, towards the next individual who dares to insult me – are all 'inside' me. These do not make very good guides either. On the contrary, if I had my wits about me I would avoid them like the plague. Rather than wondering how these things managed to get inside me in the first place, I might be wiser to ask how this notion of 'inside' me and 'outside' me first got started.

But even that looks like a bit of a waste of time in the light of responsible action, which I might right away try for, in intentional ignoration of all that pretends to be outside or inside me with a supposed right to direct and guide my behaviour.

Looking outside or inside myself for anything at all, helpful or otherwise, implies a lack of temperament. Nothing is to be learned there. Nothing really exists there. I am using these terms 'outside' and 'inside' in a strict sense, that should be kept in mind. Of special importance is, that not only is 'outside myself' a non-starter, but also, and for the same reason, so is 'inside myself'. Keep in mind, we are not talking about anything outside the house or inside a box, but outside and inside myself or yourself. And remember that anyone who is in fact guided from out- or inside himself is not very likely to agree right away with what I would call a responsible point of view. He does not – and in fact one cannot – respond to anything from outside or inside oneself.

But let us move on. A rudimentary application, or better – *exercise* of temperament could be described as a response, by me, to something 'within' of 'without' myself. Now, suddenly, a great deal has changed. I am not any more the one I was when I was guided from outside or inside myself, that is the first thing to take into consideration, and secondly, whatever I now regard as 'within' or 'without' myself has nothing whatsoever in common with anything inside or outside myself. It is as if, thanks to temperament, I had stepped into a context that is meaningful to me and to others, whereas previously I struggled ignorantly as part of a world where I might have thought well of myself, while in actual fact I was lost to myself and to others. What I called 'me' was a self indifferentiable from anything else. I can see that now, however at the time I had no notion of it, and if you had read to me what is written on these pages I would have given you a strange look. Of course there were ever so many people in the same predicament as I was; I 'bought from them and sold to them', shall we say, and for all appearances we had something in common. Alas, it was a delusory bond that united us – and it broke. Happily it occurred to me to respond to one thing or another, because on account of that the delusory nature of that bond, of that understanding and convention that we called society, became obvious and plain. I am not saying that it did not come as a bit of a shock; some times were traumatic. However the difference between the 'before' and the 'after', and especially the quality of the 'after' and the lack of quality of the 'before' became remarkable to me and I had to admit to a totally new interest now. I was being stimulated. My life had become 'stimulating'. I experienced a joy in responding to these various stimuli. Where did these stimuli originate? Certainly not outside or inside myself. I could make the comparison, and no, the stimulus-response interaction included me at all times. I was always 'with' the out and the in, and I could not any more, in all honesty and decency, accredit an outside or an inside of my self, as previously.

Mind you, it seemed possible for me to lose track of the value or quality I had discovered. Slipping back into that previous state of affairs did however, thankfully, seem quite horrible to me. Horror is the closest description of it. So it lay in my interest, in my new interest, to continue to behave responsibly and to continue to remain alert to stimuli from without and within me, and in addition to that there was this horror which set in as soon as I lost track of my best interests. I learned to interpret that horror as a positive sign and encouragement. But most importantly, I began to concentrate on what was to be gained by way of responsible interaction.

In short, <u>discipline</u> occurred to me as a useful habit to acquire. I was beginning to take advantage of my temperament. My temperament was beginning to take form.

Mature learning, then, begins for us as soon as we allow ourselves to be stimulated from without and from within. We allow that, but naturally we will not allow it while we suppose that something coming towards us and capable of moving us may do us harm. We may, out of fear, insist on remaining unmoved, and die. Sometimes it seems to hurt to be moved. We 'learn' to associate pain with internal and external stimuli, wrongly assuming that these stimuli are arrows that pierce us, from without, as the words or deeds of an enemy; from within as scruples, bad conscience, despair. "Here comes another bad mood, a depression," we say, alarmed, and our spirits sink because – our spirits sink.

What this means is that we have the wrong notion of pain, and due to that, the 'within' has slipped back into an 'inside'. In the case of that insulting person or those onerous circumstances, the without had degenerated into an 'outside'. Due to a lack of discipline, or of the right sort of discipline, we have begun to misconceive, where previously we did not conceive at all.

Disciplined learning, on the contrary, begins to unite us with what lies without us and with what lies within us. We learn of how we are in truth connected with and related to that which cannot help but seem outside or inside us when we lose track of that relation and when we stop creating that bond.

And we learn to deal with pain in a disciplined fashion. We refuse to allow ourselves to be frightened by discomfort, by rejection, by inconvenience. There we see into the heart of discipline, and here we exercise a discipline of the heart. We are often confused about the difference between the 'without' and the 'within'. We experience the weather, we notice how our inward disposition alters with the climate. Strange mood swings occur to us for no apparent reason and due to no discernible cause, but we reject the notion outright now that something outside us has caused something inside us, or the reverse. We remind ourselves and one another that pain, and fear of pain, make that error occur in us – or not, if we discipline our thinking and feeling. We learn to suffer pain rather than remaining in pain. We learn to suffer one another's pain, all in the interest of this new discovery of ours, which is our responsibility. This ability to respond has given us a taste for freedom. We have tasted the truth and liked it. In a disciplined fashion we repeatedly do combat with such inclination to let disease dictate our thought processes, and we insist on ease. In a disciplined way, as disciples of the truth, we recognise despair for what it is and insist on exceeding gladness.

And all this time we discern – we take pains to discern – the particular impulses that visit us. Unless we discern these impulses, from without and from within, we will be caught napping. An undiscerned impulse is a pain. Know that, and take the responsibility for what ails you. Certainly some things can injure you, such as false doctrines or lorries on the road, but only if you allow them to slip outside or inside you, as phenomena, while you exist in a dream, mesmerised by the magic you encourage absentmindedly. A false teaching cannot harm you while you discern the effect it has on you, because then you learn to look for true teaching instead, while the false one leaves you unaffected.

At the same time, while you cultivate a positive, friendly attitude towards fear and trembling, and while you sharpen your wits on the messages that arrive on your doorstep all day, you also discriminate: between the 'without' and the 'within', first of all because that identifies them, as response-complexes, as impulse-data, as origins of quality, of value, as sources of meaning, while you learn to cope, to understand, to deal with the actual business of your and no one else's existence. Before you learn to manage your own business you have no business meddling in the existence of others. Unless

12

you learn to differentiate thoroughly between that which goes on *without* you and that which goes on *within* you, you cannot make progress. Because a decision has to be made here. You obviously want to do something. You want to act. If you only want to contemplate your human nature, that is still, in this sense, something you do. And the thing to come to terms with here is that anything we do, any action that is going to be effective, has to start, has to be rooted, within you.

This is why we draw so much attention to the discriminating faculty, to distinction between that which is without you, such as *all the world*, and that which is within you, which is *your human being*.

Decide now to turn away, for the time being, from the world, without you, and towards your human being, within you. Here you make contact with yourself, with me, with other human beings and with god. Not bad, for a start. Not a bad decision to make. A good one, actually. You have done good. If ever you wonder what it means to do good: there is the start of it.

Temperament takes you to that point of contact, always and again. Discipline in the face of nonsense, discernment of impulses from without and from within, especially in comparison to meaningless data from outside and inside yourself, and discrimination between what goes on without you and what goes on within you, so that you can then, in actual fact, turn towards your human being and begin to do good. We might even decide to use the word 'action' for something else. We will come around to that as soon as we have had a good long and hard look at temperament.

It begins, does *temperament*, when we get fed up with being a plaything of fate and circumstance, a slave of our own shortcomings, a victim of all sorts of forces over which we have no control, and it ends, or rather its specific task comes to its conclusion, when we do good. As soon as we have turned towards our human being within us, the specific thing we mean by temperament has been accomplished.

Of course we need this faculty all the time. We do not suddenly one day in our existence begin to do good and then we do good from then on, never again to get into mischief. Reality is just not like that. We encounter those who have no notion now, nor have they perhaps ever had one, of doing good. The are lost, trapped within their own irresponsibility and possibly very unhappy about it. That misery of theirs contaminates us, and so it should because, after all, we do want to help them. If we did not experience, in our own flesh, their misery at feeling worthless and at experiencing their existence as meaningless, how could we do them good? We could not. But our doing good – our good doing – though it begins with our turning towards our human being within, must continue with our turning towards one another.

And here is something very important to keep in mind. For one thing, we cannot do good for any period of time exclusively within ourselves. Also, when we turn towards one another we do not break the contact which we have established within ourselves, with our human being within us.

We establish ourselves, we take hold, we take root – within ourselves, in our human being. In other words, we become human beings.

To be a *human being*, in this sense, means to be able to do good and to be able to do others good.

And only then, once we are established within ourselves fairly securely and when we have acquired a few good habits of sympathy, compassion and ... well, of being able and willing to take on board some problems and difficulties that have to do, principally, with others – only then does it make sense for us to turn also to the world, and to act.

At that moment, when the time has come for us to act, we might decide to teach. In the realm of action, which is, by the

14

way, never overpopulated, some are teachers. Others are writers. Still others are preachers. There are many options in the realm of reality.

10

Action is creative. While we act, we are not aware of any distinction, for us, between anything within or without us.

Remember that we have defined action as our effect, specifically, on the world. While we are effective like this, that is to say: while we act, in the true sense of the word we mean now, we are both anchored in our human being within ourselves and at the same time, on account of that, linked with other human beings. We can call this a communal link, and it exists for us for no other reason than that we are at home, inwardly, in our human being. When we now talk to others, and when we have to do with them in any way, we cannot help but communicate with them, because of this pre-established link, which itself is implied by the fact that you in your case, and I in mine, are human beings in the sense of being inwardly at home.

So I want to distinguish here between my turning towards you and welcoming you, on one hand, and on the other, my being at home in my human being, temperamentally secure. This distinction is important, because I might suppose I could do you good while I am not secure in my human being. Or I might assume that I can forever be happy and contented inwardly occupied, exclusive of you. But we have already mentioned that this is not feasible. Neither one of these is possible. If I try to be of use to you while I am divorced from the centre of my being I turn into a meddler, a busybody, and possibly a dictator and a tyrant. If, on the other hand, I am so happy and contented with myself within the confines of my individual humanity that I reject you as a disturbance, I destroy that very humanity and break the link implied by my inward being. As a consequence I lose my humanity and become popular. Or I falsify my humanity and become a crank. Popularity comes about due to my insisting on keeping you at arm's length or more by dealing with you exclusively in terms of mere appearances. By crankiness I simply mean the unwillingness to share one's human being, or more specifically the pleasure of one's human being, with others.

It would seem therefore that we are well advised to be aware of this distinction between our general link with other human beings, or simply with others, at home each one in himself and herself, and the welcoming openness to others in a way that allows them, as possible in the particular, to take advantage of our human being.

We are speaking of doing good here, not of action. Doing good means extending our good will to others and making sure that we have good will to extend. It means thought and feeling that is true and genuine, sincere, conscientious and responsible, and thinking and feeling for others, considerately and carefully. Doing good means both of these. Therefore doing good necessitates an awareness of both, and an awareness of the risks we run by becoming, so to speak, one-sided or unbalanced in that sense. When we do lose our perspective and either become attached, even addicted, to private pleasures or else become heedless, even careless, of our inward human being, we are put in mind of this somehow. We get a reminder, either from without or from within, that something is amiss or that we have been remiss. These reminders obviously have to be understood properly and interpreted correctly. In intensity they vary, from the gentle hint to the punishing interruption of our existence which can turn us into mental or physical invalids.

Basically these reminders are to return us to our communal human being. They are themselves merciful, and so much depends on our understanding of that. There is a great deal we can do in order to get back to our communal human being, and there is equally a great deal we can do to help others who are not able or willing to comprehend these merciful reminders. Only those cannot be helped who insist on their error. They condemn themselves in that way, and with respect to them we must for the time being stand by idle.

We are still concerned here with the sphere of good doing and doing good, not with the realm of real action. Our emphasis remains for the time being on this sphere – with its two hemispheres – because when things go wrong here, action cannot take place. Real action is something that either arises spontaneously out of good doing or else it grinds to a halt. Something else takes over then, which feels like action, or looks like it, or is popularly even required as action, but amounts, in reality, to nothing and often to less than nothing, which is scandalous and shameful, while all the while being popularly lauded and furtively admired.

So, although teaching is an action, and education involves teaching, we are in no rush to apply ourselves to that particular aspect of education, because we are all too aware of what passes for teaching in the popular mind and what is passed on as teaching in schools where this sphere of 'doing good', as we discuss it here, is largely neglected or even rendered impossible by standard procedure.

Now while doing good is something that pertains to each and every human being, we are all the same discussing it here in a way that would make it most relevant to someone interested in education, in teaching and learning seen as a specific, artful way of doing good. All real action is, of course, such a specific and artful way of doing good, including the writing I am doing at this moment. But, as we have already intimated, education makes sense only if teaching is understood as action in the particular.

The usual difficulty might just be acknowledged here. A real world can be envisioned, or imagined, certainly, without schoolhouses, without classrooms and without a curriculum. But a world imagined without education, without learning and teaching, is not a real world. Such an image or vision would involve a misunderstanding of children and immature adults. Only in the case of a mature adult can we speak of a learning and teaching that is not then, strictly speaking, educational, and for that reason we distinguish, only to some extent, between formal and non-formal education, in recognition of the fact that non-formal education is only loosely speaking still education but all the same teaching and learning, while formal education definitely involves an element of *intervention*, by one human being in the existence of another. This element of intervention makes perfect good sense when we apprise ourselves accurately of the nature of the child and of the predicament of the immature adult, but it becomes meaningless as soon as we contemplate mature learning and the teaching that allows it to take shape. Our *maturity*, for example, is not at risk while we take upon ourselves the pain of another and sympathise with his suffering; on the contrary, in that direction maturity remains stable, so that immaturity does not set in. But during that mature exchange with another, teaching goes on and we learn, though we ourselves are not, strictly speaking, being educated.

We will return to this difficulty at other times, and ask ourselves whether it makes any useful sense to differentiate between education on one hand and teaching/learning on the other, between formal and non-formal education. As I write this doctrine I leave my own self open to instruction.

11

Let's occupy ourselves even now with this *element of intervention* that seems to be part and parcel of what is meant by education, specifically by the education of children and immature adults.

We know that a child cannot become an adult, cannot become responsible, unless he has the help of a mature adult. And the child cannot ask the adult for help because he only feels a longing, a desire and an urge. In the absence of a mature adult's vision and supervision, that child would become a slave to his longing, a victim of his urge and an invalid of desire. How many adults are just that! And how much of each one of us is caught up by such slavery, is invalid and victimised, due to a lack of that truly mature adult impulse from within and from without!

But how, and to what extent, can an adult actually intervene? He knows of this longing, of this urge and desire in the child; elsewhere we mentioned the want to be educated. He is also aware of how this want can be mortified, how the child can be stupefied rather than enlightened, how the child can be actively misled rather than carefully guided, and how, left to his own devices, the child will automatically 'spoil', since he will not only be left with his want for education unaddressed but even with his desire for being brought up unsatisfied. Hence corruption must set in.

He looks at an actual child, then, this adult, and asks himself: "To what extent has the want for education been mortified in this child?" and in order to get an answer to that question he must *intervene*. In what does he intervene? Simply in the impersonal individuality of the child. And how does he intervene? By way of his own personality or personhood.

Certainly any adult can address any child in terms of whatever personality that child is capable. Unless one has in mind specifically to educate a child, one honours, during any attempt at communication, the actual, or even the potential, personality of that child. One undertakes to engage with that child's articulate, communicable being. That *brings the child up*. We are assuming here that the adult is more capable of personality than the child. If the opposite were the case, the child would literally be bringing up the grown-up.

We come to the difference between *education* and *upbringing* here. Upbringing involves no element of intervention. Ordinarily when I speak to a child, or have to do with him in any way, perhaps as a parent, I set him a simple example of adulthood by addressing him as a potential and real person. The effect of a *parental adult*, that is to say, of an adult who has the welfare of the child in mind during a common experience, is such that the child grows up. The appeal is to any personality of which the child might be capable.

So the child grows up by imitating and following good examples, and he is brought up by those who set those examples. All that we mean by upbringing and by growing up is exemplary. Due to the grownup, something worthwhile becomes available and the child appropriates it.

We learn a great deal about education by comparing it to an upbringing.

The educator appeals not to the personality, but to the individuality of the child. He literally bypasses whatever personality exists and ignores what might exist, while he brings his own individuality to bear on that of the child.

12

As the teacher intervenes in the individuality of the child, that child, technically, becomes a pupil. A unique human relationship exists now, between teacher and pupil, and the teacher is quite aware that due to this relationship something unusual, something extraordinary goes on – and is possible – between him and the pupil.

And now of course the teacher realizes that this awareness is crucial. He does not allow himself to forget that he and the pupil stand in a special relation to each other, and that on account of his awareness of this relation the pupil's mortified individuality is revealed to him. He discovers in what way that child's natural development has been thwarted, and at the same time he notices in himself the occurrence of a remedy.

13

Now when we speak of natural development, of individuality and personality, we might well be speaking of everything and nothing. Meaning has to be clarified. By the child's individuality we mean the way he is unique and has something to offer that no one else can offer. Our reason for getting to know someone at all is so that our individuality and his might join in *community*. This community is a marvellous way to be and should not be confused with society. Only if we understand community in some way can we appreciate the importance of individuality. Imagine the various quite different ingredients that go into the making of a delicious soup. The culinary art is what we mean by personality, where a person is aware of community as precious, and he prizes all true individuality that goes into the creation of it.

When we first discover that we are individual, and that our human nature has individual traits, we may be overjoyed, because we sense our capacity and potential for community, or we may be dismayed, because we sense the exact opposite, namely our lack of capacity and potential for community. Usually what happens is that one experiences a mixture of both and this is due to the fact that one's individuality is to some extent personally available, for communication, but also and at the same time falsified and wrong to some degree. So we are at one and the same time appalled by how inept we are and cheered by the fact that to some extent we are able to express for others who we are and what we amount to.

Now from this angle of consideration, we can see that, given equal degrees of mortification, the more educated one among us will be the one with more cause for good cheer, and the less educated one will more painfully be put in mind of how unavailable his individuality is for communication and of what a gap exists, for him, between the part of himself that ought to be expressed by him and his skill for expressing it. He experiences a definite pressure – a depression – on the side of himself that is underdeveloped or misshapen. Instead of 'misshapen', let us at this stage, instead, speak of 'deformed'. Both have to do with what we mean by mortification.

However, a distinction has to be made between that part of the child's individuality that might have been, but is not yet, developed and some other part which has been distorted. During the teacher/pupil relationship, which exists due to the teacher's 'intervention' (a key term) and on account of the teacher's specific awareness, these two elements become observable to the teacher. He detects what has been distorted and he sees what has been neglected.

14

It might seem, on the surface, that the neglect and the distortion become apparent to the teacher whether or not he decides then to do something about them, but on the contrary, the distortion and the neglect of the pupil's individuality do not become apparent until a teacher exists who has created a teacher/pupil relationship, which implies that teacher's *care* for the pupil. Such a thing as *mere* observation is not possible for the teacher. We know already that if he noticed himself becoming critical of the pupil or of himself, that would mean to him that the pedagogic relationship stands in need of repair.

On the other hand, the intervention is not possible except, in the most specific sense of that word: carefully. Unless the adult *takes care*, he cannot even become a practicing teacher.

15

What we would like to show now is how a careful intervention does in fact become a welcome experience for the child. Let's keep in mind that a child is a pupil only while in that practical relationship with a careful teacher. We cannot take for granted that in the common experience of a conventional schooling every child looks forward to the effect any designated member of the teaching staff of that school has on him. The way things just happen to be in our neighbourhood is a matter of opinion, but a doctrine is valuable on account of the inroads it allows us to make on the truth due to the way we feel and think.

So the fact that the teacher bypasses any personality of the child during the course of this intervention has to be understood in the light of what that teacher has in mind, of his reason for doing it. We know how all our actions are made, marred or even undone by whether our reason for doing them, of for our acting in the first place, is sufficient, insufficient, or even absent. Only because the teacher knows what he is doing does the child respond as pupil – and in that word 'pupil' we find hidden the very secret of an as yet unexplored individuality, and of an individuality that should be and might be communicable.

Compare this for a moment to what is described in a certain literary context familiar to many of us, where someone says to 'disciples', not pupils, "my words have cleansed you". Here too the implication seems to be, that a change has been brought about by a 'master', in a 'disciple', within a certain master/disciple relationship, and that this is a change which compares to a cleansing, to a removal of unwanted 'matter'– so that something else, something outside and beyond that relationship can take place.

This brings us around to the notion of education as principally a rendering of individuality capable of personality, so that the *pedagogic intervention* has as its aim the cleansing, or liberation, of the young individuality of all the effects of mortification, of neglect and distortion, for the sake and purpose of the freedom which then becomes accessible, or at least more accessible.

We need to keep in mind that not all of a given child's individuality has become mortified. This is as important as our realizing that some of it may be in need of 'being cleansed'. We can use our own words to describe this.

There are those in whom we cannot, with the best of will, detect any individuality at all. It's almost as if they were conspiring with their deadening circumstances in the destruction of their individuality, so as to – what 'reason', why? Has expression been too painful? Have attempts at communication been too cruelly thwarted? Why would anyone prefer the non-existence of the popular masses to individual communication among human beings?

We are not far enough into this doctrine to deal with the so-called 'autistic child' or with 'manic-depressive' behaviour in immature adults, but our notion of individuality and of pedagogic intervention must allow for them, not only as explanation but primarily as remedy.

We feel moved, therefore, to posit something, in one another, as individuality which, in the case of a creative adult human being, is indifferentiable from personality. That which you as a creative person express is your individuality, and the two, your personality and your individuality, are respectively something like means and substance. And it has to be seriously considered that it makes no sense to speak of the two as in any sense distinguishable during creative action. True personality communicates what is individual. A person in action makes an individual contribution. A personal communication is also individual. And so on.

Now in order to make this configuration of individuality and personality useful for our discussion of the pedagogic intervention, we have to emphasize that a teacher/pupil relationship is out of place except where individuality and personality are distinguishable. A pedagogic intervention is not even possible where creative humanity is in play. I think we could safely say that creative action, which is after all only possible in responsible freedom, is the behaviour of a fully educated human being. Similarly we can of course say that such responsible freedom – and the creative action that ensues from it and supports it – is *the goal of all education.* We have arrived here at the upper limit of the educational purpose, where we step back, as educators, and pray that our charges will in fact be creative now outside the pedagogic relationship. We have given them a taste for freedom. Will they bite into the fruit? Will they offer nourishment to others?

16

So the caring teacher intervenes where a gap exists, a gap distinguishable to him, between a pupil's individuality and personality, and his reason for this intervention, as seen from our present vantage point, is the beneficial effect he intends to have on the individuality of his pupil insofar as that individuality has been distorted and neglected. Of course if he knows about neglect in this area, he also understands that the individual nature of every human being is a reality difficult to overestimate. Something exists here which is waiting, under the best of circumstances, to be led out, to be drawn forth, to be wooed into the light of day. The teacher takes the fullest possible account of the fact that circumstances have not been of the best, hence the distortion and the neglect, the signs of which stare him in the face now. But he does not take issue with these negatives. He notes them, he takes stock of them, with his thinking mind and his feeling body, but he does not take issue with them, he does not even confront them except to deny them access to what he does eventually allow for, and that is the sane and sound individuality of his pupil which he rightly welcomes as 'something' that actually waits to be led out into the light of day.

As soon as the intervening teacher makes contact with the sane and sound individuality of his pupil, his intervention stops because he has arrived at his goal. And here now suddenly something very exciting happens. What the teacher, for the purpose of his pedagogic intervention, has posited as individuality, has become indistinguishable from – from the child. Not from the pupil, but from the young human being, the child.

But of course this sane and sound child stands revealed to – the teacher, and within the pedagogic context. What does the teacher do now, since his intervening activity has achieved its goal?

He simply goes on to the next step, which is not intervention and not even an activity, but a *passivity*, and in fact a passivity that can be called *guidance*.

The task that teacher sets himself now is the guidance of that child through the maze of individually incurred mortifications with which the teacher has, during the course of his intervention, become familiar even to the point of compassion with the pupil on account of them.

17

As a guide, the teacher is passive. Also, as a guide he has to do with a child, not with a pupil. What difference does it make to him that he observes this distinction?

The purpose of the intervention has been to get to know the child. However, once he knows the child, the teacher still has the pupil in mind. He must do, otherwise education stops, and the pupil falls back under the mortifications of his individuality. But the teacher cannot explain to the pupil in so many words what these mortifications, made up of neglect and distortions, are, so as to let the child deal with them in future. If the child had what it takes to deal with them, he would not have been mortified in the first place.

So this presents a great problem to the teacher. This problem might be formulated in some way successfully if we point to the need now, insofar as the child is concerned, for a parental adult. The question is: Can that particular teacher be a parental adult?

Awkward circumstances sometimes dictate complicated means. It won't do if we pretend that human beings nowadays need a simple solution to a straightforward problem. One feels tempted to suggest: The child's natural urge to grow up and be responsible has been falsified and wronged – very well, the teacher undoes the damage and hands the child back to ideal parents.

But there are no ideal parents. When the teacher gets to know the child after becoming acquainted with the child's various complexes and hang-ups, he cannot help seeing how these were 'brought about' by the times in which we all live. He notices how the apparent parents of the child practically encourage such mortifications. The so-called parents are themselves immature adults, in dire need of education, so how can they be expected to guide their child towards mature adulthood? And of course even in himself does any teacher worth his salt know of a myriad tendencies to immaturity and of inclinations to irresponsibility. There is only one perfect teacher and very few know of him. Those who know of him are of course endowed with a singular advantage because of what they know they can leave to him. They inwardly know their own teacher, and little by little they manage to pass this knowledge of the one teacher of all human beings on, tentatively and tacitly.

18

Now here we have come to a point in our doctrine where we have to advance more carefully than ever because the topic we touch on is surrounded by controversy and undermined by indifference. Indeed one hesitates to touch on it because of the immense amount of misunderstanding and misinformation that clouds this issue of what we shall call 'the

27

teacher of all mankind in our hearts'. A phrase like that seems 'safe' enough, safe in the sense of unprovocative, but right away the clamour arises: Whom does he mean, who is that teacher? And what has he to do with a doctrine of education? Is an otherwise perfectly sensible discussion to deteriorate into a dialectic of metaphysics and mysticism? We are having a tricky enough time holding together the two halves of theory and practice. Are we to be confronted now by a personalized belief-system where we imagined good will and common sense would suffice?

But exactly there, at those two points of good will and common sense, I would like to make contact for the next section of our doctrine, as we undertake to deal fairly and squarely with the singular predicament of teachers nowadays, who are to 'guide children' once they have become familiar with their 'pupils' in the sense of the caring intervention we previously described. And in order for this contact to hold, we can do one of two things. Either we must allow for some force or energy under which all human beings, children and parents, pupils and teachers, adults and grown-ups alike, are bound to labour and endure, in a hard world where the fittest survive or else suffer the consequences – or: we may avail ourselves of the good will and common sense of this teacher of all mankind in our hearts who informs us of what we wish to know at a time when we are ready to benefit from such knowledge in a world forever open to creation and discovery.

Now the first of these <u>must</u> be. There is pressure on us aplenty to confirm that choice. But really it amounts more to a giving-in, than to a choice. There is nothing choice about a hard world where survival is the goal and the ego triumphs unless drugged by magical artistry and inhibited by manmade laws.

The second must not be, but <u>may</u> be, and it is most definitely a choice. However we cannot understand what it amounts to until we have chosen it, although everywhere we look we can see such a crying need for it that on that account alone we might choose rather than give in.

19

Perhaps we have not identified the problem sufficiently. It has to do with the predicament of the teacher who has managed to become familiar with his pupil to the point where he can see the true individuality of the pupil, distinct from those aspects of the individuality that have been, so to speak, compassionately absorbed by the teacher, so that now that teacher is in contact with the child as seen distinct from the pupil. The pupil is in that pedagogic relation with the teacher, where we spoke of a mix of individualities and where the teacher repeatedly interprets resistance compassionately and hatred lovingly. He lavishes care on the pupil whatever his feelings and opinions are in association and contact with the pupil. Nothing puts the teacher off and he refrains from judgment, condemnation and criticism, even from applause and praise, all in the interest of that part of the pupil's individuality which is still unspoiled and straight. He knows as soon as he does make contact with the true child; there is a peace and a true sense of understanding. Also, as the teacher may learn to his own surprise the first few times, the pedagogic relation as such is not any more identifiable or appropriate to be maintained. Should the teacher stop being a teacher? Is there such a thing as a child/teacher relationship? We have already ascertained that what the true child needs is a guide.

Keep in mind here that what we mean by the true child is known, at that moment, by the teacher, as he has to do, outwardly, with what to all intents and purposes is still his pupil. Only inwardly has he made contact with something greater than his pupil, namely this true child. He sees it as his task now that this true child should gradually be brought out into the light of day so as to become a mature adult, eager for responsibility. On first acquaintance that true child, as inwardly recognized by the teacher, is a young human being more than ever ready to grow up and wishing to grow up, and now at last at liberty to grow up, thanks to the teacher.

The difficulty for us is that we find it awkward to imagine how the teacher could be aware at once of the latent pupil and the actual child. He is aware outwardly of the pupil and inwardly of the true child. The difficulty for the teacher, however, lies in the problem of how to relate this true child to everyday circumstances when all around those conditions prevail that initially 'caused' the neglect and distortion of the child's individuality before he became a pupil.

But then we should call to mind here that those everyday circumstances conditioned the child negatively, or were able to have that mortifying effect on the child's individuality, only because the child's desire to grow up, to mature, had not been sufficiently, or adequately addressed.

So the teacher, as soon as the becomes inwardly aware of the child's true, unspoiled and unimpaired individuality, has also within his grasp that same child's natural desire to mature. And to this he may respond now as a guide. Does he begin to do something now that would not have been appropriate before? Does he stop doing something that would not be appropriate now?

The intervention stops and the guidance begins.

20

The true child looks up to the teacher as to someone whose influence is good. Not that the teacher needs to do anything to earn the true child's trust. It suffices that the teacher be who he is, namely the one who in terms of good will and common sense maintains a barrier, initially, between the true child and any further mortification.

In the presence of the teacher as guide, the child learns first of all to appreciate what it means to be at liberty. The courage to exist becomes a distinct experience. So does the hope for a useful future. We cannot ignore, that prior to the beginning of its education, and even while the child's up-bringing was perhaps well in hand, some attachments had formed which the child could not possibly have properly understood but which fell into that category of false desire, wrong motivation and bad habit which interposed itself between the true child and his real adulthood. How the teacher stands, in person, between these hindrances and the child and says, as it were, to the child: "Trust me as I protect you against these hindrances while you grow. Left to your own devices you would once again be confused buy what happens within you. Your nature would be overshadowed by its own products, of which you as yet know very little, if anything. You nature is an active principle, a dynamic source. You have within yourself the energy what will either become mischief or strength. My task is to help you become aware of that energy in such a way that you will recognize it without falling prey to it. A distance has to be created between you who know and your self that is profitably overcome. Until now you have not been acquainted with this discrepancy between yourself as truthful and your self as a misleading force – misleading if you do not overcome it. You, as one who overcomes, and your self, as that which you overcome – these two I would teach you now. I can do it in many ways. I can do it by personal example. I can point to other examples of it. I can encourage you to do it, for example."

21

If this is the inward disposition of the teacher, the true child cannot help but trust him. The child will "hear his voice".

But how does the teacher maintain this disposition, and how does he sustain himself under the burden of all that his pupil 'hands over' to him now?

We must recognize that something is transferred, and the teacher knows that something is transferred. Something that burdened the child and the child did not know it, now burdens the teacher, and the teacher knows it. The teacher does what is necessary to recognize the burden transferred from his pupil and now resting on himself. His attitude towards this burden is crucial, because on it depends whether the true child is guided or – betrayed.

Imagine now a teacher with a number of pupils, and in the case of most of these pupils the teacher has progressed to the point where the true child has been contacted and a burden, which for the time being we shall call a burden of distrust, is being transferred. The collective burden which rests on the teacher is appreciable. The two senses of that word 'appreciable' stand us in good stead here. Because the burden is being described as something that mounts up <u>and</u> as something that can be dealt with – by way of appreciation.

22

We may imagine the teacher as the carrier of a collective burden of mistrust. We call it mistrust because it prevented the pupils, at one time, from trusting the teacher.

What matters now is that the teacher be a willing carrier of this burden. Not that he feels that his pupils mistrust him. What he does feel is a paralysis of his willpower. He cannot make sense in the particular of what it is that causes something like a blank of his mind and a heaviness of his body, and he knows that it would not at all be useful to look for such a cause, for he carries the burden of his pupils. He makes that intelligent connection in his mind, between an inward condition that prevents him from functioning in a predictable way, and an outward state of liberty enjoyed by his pupils.

Not for long does this burden depress the teacher. He indentifies it correctly. He is careful not to shrug the burden off by indulging in unrelated activity, and he refuses to offload it by blaming pupils, himself or circumstances for it. He identifies the burden correctly as that which signals the beginning of his activity as a guide.

He does not shrug off or offload the burden, but he carries it, and he carries it out. This is a matter of will, and of willpower. More than that, it is a case of good will. When the teacher comes up with good will in the event of such a burden of mistrust on his shoulders he sets an example as a guide. He does something that his pupils find irresistible. Since he waits, for this exercise of good will, until he is burdened, his good will is powerful, for it overcomes his own tendency and inclination to distrust in reaction.

Meanwhile, outwardly, the teacher makes use of common sense. All those activities that enliven a classroom in the interest of the curriculum are based on that rare commodity called common sense. Imagine what all our senses have in common. Consider the meaning we all share in common. There is really a great deal of it. And here begins the teacher's task of describing various aspects of the world in the light of this common sense, outwardly visible and not at all hidden. Whatever he selects as material suitable for the pupil's appreciation he presents outwardly, visibly and plainly, and his test for this is that it may not interfere with his inward awareness of his burden and of his active power of good will.

So both inwardly and outwardly the teacher as guide is occupied. And he insists that these two areas of activity should not in any way become obscured. If suddenly the teacher notices that the outward/inward awareness has given way to an inside – outside confrontation, involving stress, nervousness and impatience, high spirits and empty enthusiasm, a routine observance of rules and regulations – all conditions and states that are one moment inside and the next moment outside and therefore to be described as one-dimensional – he calls a halt and takes himself to task. He realises that he has stopped being a guide and allowed himself to become a mechanism. The twofold state of awareness must be re-established before he proceeds.

He begins by turning inward, to assure himself of his reason for being a teacher. He contemplates his motivation. He is on safe ground here, since he knows himself predisposed to his profession. Gradually his awareness returns. He knows who he is. And he would like his pupils to know who he is. For a time he had strayed, instead of being a guide. He had strayed in the sense of pretending to teach at one moment and then suffering a spell of fatigue. Then he did something energetic to raise his spirits, only to fall into a slump of self-accusation. Then he was annoyed, and then he dealt out punishment. One time he was outside himself, then he was inside. He can see it clearly, now that he has returned to who he is, namely a guide to his pupils who inwardly carries the burden that has been transferred to him and who outwardly makes distinct common sense of some selected aspects of the world.

23

From the point of view of a teacher, it is important to be able to recognize that state of unwillingness that comes along with the burden of mistrust that is every creative teacher's lot. The twofold awareness allows for that state, so that we do not pronounce upon it, override it energetically or condemn in terms of it, but we see it simply and practically as an opportunity for coming up with good will on our part. It is not what one automatically does. No one carries his burden automatically. No one ever has done that. It is not enough to be conscious. We have to be aware. And only after long practice do we become 'professional' in the sense that we regard our 'teacher's burden', the burden of the guide, dispassionately, as the sort of hardship we do after all expect. Along with that acceptance comes a much greater facility, of course, for instituting good will. But we should never suppose that we can make a routine of this good will and never again experience the paralysis of mistrust, on our faculties and even on ourselves. This would be a great mistake, and is often made where such a thing as 'pure thought' is entertained as a separate, practical possibility. When a teacher makes that mistake he presumes he can be greater than his own teacher, and then when mercifully, but contrary to all his vain expectations, pain and hardship set in, he must blame and condemn, himself or others. He calls that a set-back and strives to get over it, so as to return to pure thought, pure will, pure feeling, whatever works best for him so that he may continue to delude himself, and often others, about the real meaning of our human burden or cross.

24

It might be a good idea to linger with this topic for a while. One question is: Do we have to wait, before we reach for the good, until something bad has to be overcome? The answer, of course, is no. We all have a fair notion of what we ourselves mean by 'the good', and quite naturally we reach for it and ask for it. We know, even, that we have to strive for it, because it won't come our way unasked. All the same, it does want to come our way. There is that in the good which is personally predisposed in our favour, and those who know that usually ask in a different manner than those who only imagine the good as dead material or as an instrumental force.

The other question that has bearing on our topic is: What are we to make of pain, death and misfortune? Are we to regard these as judgment on our past behaviour? Are we to say: If only I had behaved differently this would not have happened? No, such an attitude is itself unfortunate. Are we to accuse and to blame others, or circumstances? Surely that amounts to the same thing. In both cases our conclusion is that if only we had behaved or done differently, the pain or misfortune might have been prevented.

And, of course again, where common sense is concerned – or where we are concerned commonsensically, if I had driven more carefully that accident probably would not have happened. Or if I had really lived, I would not have died. And that still leaves pain. Traditional philosophers do not come to terms with pain. The dead, presumably, lead a painless existence, like automatons, but those who prefer to live come up against pain. There is pain of the spirit and of the flesh, of the mind and of the body, indeed of our very soul itself. When I myself am in pain, not to mention some part of myself, I cannot even think straight. There is a distinct tendency to despair.

So naturally I am tempted sooner or later to think in such a way that pain can never touch me again. I am tempted to invent a type of thought that will remove me above and beyond those pain-sensitive parts and areas of myself. If anyone comes along and promises me even the possibility of such a thought, I am tempted to listen and believe. It won't matter to me so much whether he calls it positive thought or pure thought, ideal or angelic thought – all the same to me, just so long as I have a tool in my hands to keep me out of the clutches of pain.

And once you take the pain out of misfortune and death, what else is there to worry about?

Usually it is a very high, an overweening spirituality, that tempts me in this fashion. It is a spirituality beyond good and evil in the common sense, and it rightly calls itself 'beyond', but only because it maintains itself in a realm assiduously removed from the human. What this spirituality means, practically, is that we can be rid of pain while still conscious, as long as we rid ourselves of the human element. Obviously it is because we are still human that pain can get at us.

Then again it is not obvious at all. Is human being, or even humanity itself, to be equated with pain? Surely not. The temptation persuades me to think of human being differently. I am to redefine it, away from the flesh, removed from matter, and imbued with something like ideal, or angelic, powers. In that way I avoid the 'human condition' altogether and may look with pity upon those who are still entangled in flesh and matter.

But of course I am at fault precisely because I mistake what it means to be human. In fact I become quite blind to the human in reality as soon as I begin to define it in terms of the ideal. There is nothing ideal about human nature. Human being is something that has to be seen to be believed. If there is anything to be gained, counter-productively, from having given in to this temptation to overweening spirituality, then it is a definition of humanity proper on its own terms. Which is a gain not to be scoffed at.

In fact, such a definition of human being is something we cannot do without in the case of creative education.

25

What we learn very rapidly when once we have recognized the danger of overweening spirituality is that it is one thing to talk about man and another to talk about human beings, such as men, women and children. Human beings are really quite marvellous inventions, and sooner or later we are bound to come to the conclusion that as human beings we are not souls, or spirits, or minds, or bodies, or flesh – but more than all of these put together. Any doctrine of education stands or falls depending on whether or not it sees human beings as quite unique in comparison to other creatures. If once we get into the habit of saying: 'twenty souls' when we mean twenty human beings we have missed an important point. A human being can lose his soul or posses his soul. He may have a spirit, he may even have a good spirit – or not. He can lose his mind, be disembodied and even be rid of his flesh – and still, technically, be a human being.

Ask yourself what you are, and if you can truthfully say: "I am a human being" you are in a privileged position. It means that you were born with a capacity for sustaining eternal life in soul, spirit and flesh. There is more to you than your soul, your spirit and your flesh – if you have these. What else is there? There is your human being.

How to be human – it is an unusual question, especially for those who insist on abiding with appearances alone. A degree of wakefulness is required before such a question an be interesting for us. Indeed there seems no better way of illustrating, that even being implies the doing of something, than if we say to someone? "Be human!".

Be human, would you, please?

I will try my best. Where shall I start? I assume I was born human, so let me go back in my mind and memory to that childhood state when not yet a great number of questionable teachings had been heaped on my head. I had a kind of wisdom, then, and I remember it still. I knew that whatever might happen to me I would always be alright. Let me say that I trusted. It came naturally to me, to trust. It came human naturally. My human birth was in trust. And that was marvellous. Today I am back where I was then, in terms of this happy trust, but it took some effort to manage. I think for a time I was hardly what I would call human today. I don't want to lose any sleep over how that distraction came about, but on account of it I can say, today, with the conviction born of experience, that human being is worthwhile. I would say that I consider it my single great ambition to be human.

And central to being human, for me, is this integrity built on trust. I cannot afford to build on any of my activities, of soul, spirit or flesh, because, again, these activities are either meaningful and worthwhile or not, depending entirely on whether or not they proceeded from this trust which I perceive as the core of my being. And, as I intimated earlier, to trust means to do something. I can trust or not trust.

So human being implies, for me, the doing of this trust. And if I now ask myself: Do I trust in spirit, in soul or in my flesh? – I can, after careful reflection, only answer: None of these. This trust does not proceed from my thinking mind or from my feeling body. It does not reside in my spirit either, because this spirit does not even belong to me unless I trust. Neither does it arise as a consequence of my contemplating soul, nor does it exist in terms of my flesh. It comes 'before' all these. It is I myself who trust, and quite distinctly from all those parts or members of me. Not until I trust do I discover that I am whole rather than a number of parts; and not until I have trusted long enough, through thick and thin, in spite of all setbacks and shortcomings and nevertheless – do I realize that as a whole human being all these 'members' are completely at my disposal. I may trust intuitively, intellectually, instinctively or intelligently, but first I must trust. I may will what I like but will not have satisfaction until I will trustingly. Then, suddenly everything comes my way.

And I do not at all hold that human beings have to acquire this trust. On the contrary, we are born with it. And if we lose it we can get it back. So it does make a difference to how I go about availing myself of something, whether I assume that it lies ready within me and needs only to be rediscovered, or whether I look for it outside myself, as something that needs to be added on to me, like a shirt or trousers.

This trust which makes out my humanity is not like a shirt or trousers. It is more like the essence of my being, if you know what I mean; and I put myself in a vulnerable position here so that you can indeed know what I mean.

26

Imagine now how difficult it must be for some to be human, if they cannot trust unless they can trust in this or that! And the woods are full of the casualties of such a qualified trust. And of course as soon as you say that you cannot trust unless you trust in this or that, you make your humanity depend on this or that, and you imply that this or that is therefore greater than you. And if you want to say that you trust in god, then you are not saying anything different from what I am saying, unless of course you are imagining the god of your choice, which I do not recommend.

27

The main difference I see here between a young and a mature human being is that the young one trusts from birth and the mature one from rebirth. A mature human being was perfectly alright at one time like a fish in water, but, since a human being is not a single state being, he had to learn to cope on dry land. He can still enjoy swimming and diving but he calls himself mature as soon as he feels at home, (as soon as the trusts) on dry land, whereupon he right away helps his young fellows to cope with that land existence, because they still hanker for the exclusive water-life, the amniotic unawareness of fresh air and direct day light.

40

Let us not overstretch the metaphor. Human beings <u>may</u> mature or they <u>must</u> mature. If they do not mature they quite simply become inhuman. In that case their humanity passes them by and discards them. It is difficult to picture this outright. I think it is important to confront the truth that anyone is at liberty to forfeit his humanity. What do we call such drop-outs from the human race? It does not matter, but we cannot call them human beings.

And here is a sobering thought, with great bearing on our understanding of education. While grownups can finally miss the boat entirely, so that there is no more hope at all for them, children can become so engrossed in their unintentional self-centricity that it becomes nearly impossible for them to be educated. The main consideration here, after all, is that for children there is always hope.

But how can an educator tell the difference between a child, with learning potential, and a grown-up who has missed the boat?

Indeed, how can anyone tell?

I suppose, the question one should really ask is: Why do you want to know? Idle curiosity has no business meddling in affairs of the heart, and human being is an affair of the heart.

Or does it boil down to the old theological chestnut: Is eternal damnation possible for a human being? No, that is a misstatement of the problem. If I forfeit my humanity I am not a human being any more. As for eternal condemnation, that is really nothing to worry about, because those who have lost their humanity can hardly be said to be in pain, so it won't do to try to scare anyone into being human, although that has been tried for almost two millennia.

As soon as we face that, we can take on board that wherever there is hope – or despair! – there we may educate. Where there is neither hope nor despair, why waste time? However, from the point of view of the seriously responsible educator, despair is as good a sign of present humanity as hope, because the teacher is concerned over only one thing, initially, and that is the existence of humanity. He does not worry himself about the absence of it, in this case or in that case. He does not say: "My God, these shells are walking around and although they look like human beings there is obviously no one at home in that housing! What am I going to do?" If he feels moved to do something, then let him go ahead, because possibly he is wrong about his assessment. If he has a go and comes up against a total blank wall, so that he experiences neither acceptance nor rejection, then let him simply turn elsewhere. He would be wasting his time. However rejection will do as well as acceptance to let him know that something worthwhile could be done here.

It tells us a lot about what human being amounts to, when we realize that no other creature or creation, animal, vegetable or mineral, can slip out of being entirely. Non-being is open only to the human specimen. This total liberty is unavoidable in our case, because we are also completely free to 'crown the creation', as it were. Since we are free to be gods, we are also at liberty to cease from being. Surely that thought has a definite and real appeal to it! It is like a breath of fresh air in our modern dungeon. And don't confuse cessation of being with cessation of life, or with the absence of life. There is hope for the dead, but not for those who have ceased from being, which is to say from humanity.

28

What we have learned from this is that in terms of the trust that defines our human being we are able to deal creatively with pain. As adults and as mature human beings we know that we are free to trust and at liberty not to trust. The distinction between liberty and freedom comes out very nicely like this. A mature adult tastes freedom when he chooses to trust in the face of his liberty not to trust. In addition to this freedom he gains the ability to deal with pain, and to deal with it intelligently and productively. It makes no difference in this case whether he deals with his own pain or, compassionately, with the pain of another. He knows that he stands to gain something each and every time. He knows pain as a harbinger of increase, even though initially it is an anxiety or a fear. Where the knowing begins, the fear stops.

Dealing creatively with pain is called suffering. It helps to illustrate what we mean by this human trust if we say that we <u>trust that</u> pain signals the availability of something good for us and we <u>trust so that</u> we are actually receptive to it. Whether the pain, the misery, the discomfort, etc. is our own or that of another, by suffering it we attain to something good and we move closer to the good and become more one with it. Notice that the good is both quantitative and qualitative.

29

In the light of what we said earlier about the overweening spirit that promises to remove us from pain if we pay for the favour with human being, we can see clearly now our real need for acknowledging our human burden. We spoke of the pupil in whom, due to the teacher's careful educational intervention, the true child was liberated from all those mortifications that had set in due, basically, to the fact that the child was not sufficiently raised. The teacher was then to become the guide of that child. We mentioned the burden which the teacher had assumed and which he chose to bear on the child's behalf, with good will, and so as to overcome his own state of unwillingness, which state invariably sets in with every new pupil.

We discussed then the very real temptation that presents itself to the teacher-as-guide, and most insistently to the best teacher, to become greater than his own teacher and master. The tempter says: "There is no need for any such burden. Stay ahead of the doubt, of the misery and of the will-paralysis by becoming like me, pure spirit. Suffering and pain are one and the same. Outstrip them. Liberate others as I liberate you. Freedom is the same as liberty. Above all addict yourself to pure thought. Set the example of the free spirit whom nothing can touch."

And this tempter of course knows nothing of suffering as an act of love, and he knows nothing of freedom as commitment and responsibility. Indeed he knows nothing of human being. One might go so far as to say that he resents it, finds it scandalous, and certainly 'impure'. He approves of us just then when as human beings we become hollow. The heroic morality disappears first, if ever there was any. Soon follows the social morality. What is left is a spectre with liberal tendencies. Such a spectre then sets itself up in front of a group of children and exercises an inhuman influence.

The way out of such a predicament is gained in terms of an understanding of what we mean by our common human lot and then by a cheerful acceptance of that lot as something that would be revealed to us as our individual human good if we but rubbed the sleep out of our eyes and took heart.

When we say now that the teacher of the pupil is to guide the child, we mean first and foremost a guidance into such a cheerful acceptance of our common human burden. We mean something that takes years, and which all the while will be contemplated by the teacher as his or her guiding principle – for herself as for her charges.

44

For where before, there was a 'mix of individualities', during the period while she was getting to know the pupil, there is now a common understanding that is based on trust.

30

In the case of the child, such understanding is only just barely beginning, and all the same we are justified in speaking of it as being in common with that of the teacher, though the teacher's is thorough.

A definite and unique communication becomes possible now between teacher and pupil. Every morning, when the pupil comes into the company of the teacher, a degree of intervention will be required until the teacher once again makes contact with the true child. This needs to take no more than a moment. Then the issue is clear, because then it becomes possible for the teacher as guide to limit himself to the specific task of ordering the collective awareness of everyone in the classroom, including herself, in terms of a burden which should now be obvious to everyone, but which is viewed creatively by the teacher and with anything from scepticism to enthusiasm by the children.

However this burden is viewed by the children, this does not particularly concern the teacher. Her main goal is that they should eventually, that day, choose to bear it. This is something very specific, and we have to look closely at it.

First of all we should look at the burden and decide on its actual composition. Quite wrong simply to point to a workload related to the curriculum. There is certainly what we called an 'aspect of the world' commonsensically viewed, by which aspect we meant the spelling, the geography, the whatever that one picks, as a teacher, as one's curricular context. This is not the burden which the child comes up against. One child, when faced with geometry exercises, feels burdened heavily, the other only very lightly. We tend to say that the first child is 'good' at geometry while the second is not good at it and finds it not easy, but hard. The creative teacher finds it much more interesting to concern himself with the second child, who is burdened, than with the first who waltzes through the exercises, because where no burden exists, the guidance, as we have defined it, cannot take place.

31

The problem for the child of course, or rather for the pupil, is that he identifies the burden he experiences with the curriculum, or even with the whole business of coming to a school, attending in class and 'not being able to do what he likes'. He sees only the work-load, as we all do when we get bogged down and become one-dimensional. The inward is not any more distinct from the outward and we are one minute inside and the next minute outside. But the teacher not only knows what the pupil's problem is, she also sees the work and the load in distinction. She knows and understands that in reality they are distinct. She acknowledges, to herself above all, how often it happens to her that she gets discouraged by 'how much there is to do', but at the same time she realizes that when that happens it must be immediately interpreted by her as an attitude problem. Her own attitude needs to be adjusted. Unless she always and again begins with that she cannot guide a child. Because guidance, for the child, means, initially, an awareness to be acquired of this difference between the work and the load. If the teacher walks around with a workload she 'has to get done', so that she can then relax and do something or be something imaginary, she is obviously not going to help the child make that crucial distinction between work and burden on which so much else depends.

And why is this distinction so important? Why does that part of education we call guidance actually depend on it?

Because the burden itself actually has to be carried. It has to be picked up, so it has to be 'seen' first of all. The workload is not the burden. The workload is psychic and trau-

46

matic. The workload is symptomatic of a lack of knowledge and understanding. When the child comes up against it there is immediate decline. Before such a workload, especially if affirmed or even enforced by grown-ups, the child goes back into hiding and one is left with a pupil who goes through the motions, sceptically or enthusiastically, depending, I dare say, on hormones.

So the workload is, in an important sense, a mistake, or a misunderstanding, but it presents the challenge to the one-dimensional existence of the pupil, so that an inward/outward awareness might come about. The pupil is to become aware himself, for the first time perhaps, of his own inward being, and then, in relation to that, of outward being. The teacher feels the struggle that is going on, as the pupil slides off this way and that way and as the child longs to come out into the open but declines before the problematic character of present experience. And the best the teacher can do is assert her own inwardness while refusing to engage with the pupil on the one-dimensional level, which is always a great temptation.

32

If the challenge of the workload is not met, the child goes into hiding. The pupil might be dealing with the so-called demands of the curriculum in a splendid fashion, he might be doing all his homework and achieving high grades, but no creative education is going on. If the pupil achieves marvellous results but the true child is asleep, so who benefits?

And yet, is that not the dream of standard education, to prepare for the job, for he profession and for the career? So the pupil learns to 'pull his weight'. The 'good' pupil pulls it willingly, pulls it charismatically – but the child declines and passes away. The attitude towards the workload is one-dimensional. There is popular success outside, of there is psychic intensity inside, and the one plays into the other. Or there is popular failure and psychic impotence. It makes no difference, because whether the pupil is 'brilliant or dull, energetic or lazy, the true child does not come out into the open. But that is what all real education should be about. Our animal tendencies can become ever so developed, but sadly at the expense of our human virtues and characteristics.

One takes the wrong route. The secondary is mistaken for the primary. That which should not be neglected becomes the main outlet and goal. There is the bad habit of judgement according to appearances, which gradually becomes ingrained. There is addiction to temporary rewards. Individuality is throttled by individualism. A personality is manufactured while personality is sacrificed. Demonic gestures become the rule while all sense and feeling for genuine behaviour is lost. A demonic indifference comes over the land like a plague and is called peace.

33

If the challenge of the workload is met, it ceases being a workload and what we suddenly have is an inward burden being borne and simultaneously an outward set of instructions, duties and demands of which the pupil is aware and against which he does not rebel. Against the workload there is always a rebellion, tacit or expressed, and then force comes into play to counteract the rebellion or the load is cast off.

Against instructions, duties and demands that are experienced as outward there is never a rebellion, because two faculties or organs come alive that allow the true child to make a preliminary move towards the light of day. There two organic faculties are observation and obedience. We have to be careful how we understand these. The best sense we can make of them comes from connecting them in our minds with that burden that is being borne, which burden the teacher bears willingly as a constant example for the child. And of course the teacher already observes and obeys. These faculties are alive in every mature human being. What we describe here is what happens as the child follows the teacher's example.

Observation and obedience then are discovered by the child at that crucial moment when his one-dimensional existence becomes two-dimensional, when the now outside and then inside existence is replaced by a simultaneous outward and inward existence and, most important, when that which is initially experienced as a workload, against which the pupil rebels, is recognized as a burden inwardly to be borne and as a set of outward instructions, duties and demands to be observed and obeyed.

The teacher simply says: "Do this and do that." Then he knows what to expect. Either there is open rebellion, where the pupil all but says no, or else there is a slavish compliance, by a pupil who is supposed to be good and whose rebellion is being entirely internalized, which is really an inside rebellion. What usually happens is a combination of both, so that unwillingness and fear are manifested, reluctance to 'get down to work' and eagerness to please the teacher. All of these are simply noted by the teacher as one-dimensional reaction to a workload. Neither does she punish for the outside rebellion, the show of unwillingness and reluctance, nor does she reward the inside rebellion, the fear and the eagerness to please. The education she intends is not standard but creative. Her specifically creative task begins now as she confronts these one-dimensional reactions, which she initially always again experiences as a workload, and turns this experience, observantly and obediently, into an inward burden for herself and an outward set of duties, demands and instructions. In other words, she does exactly, and in actual reality, and on the spot in front of the pupil, what she would like the pupil to do. In that way she is a true guide now. As soon as she made use of the pupil-teacher relationship by 'telling what to do' the child felt addressed and made ready to observe and to obey, but could not, because of the pupil's understandable reaction. If this one-dimensional reaction is encouraged by the teacher, if she rewards the pupil's eagerness to please or approves of his fear, or if she aggravates the rebellion of the pupil through use of force, punishment and condemnation, then the child declines again and remains hidden, neglected and rejected, which is to say: mortified. But if the teacher behaves creatively, by 'facing the wolf', then the wolf cannot tear the child, and the child fallows the guide, by following the example of two-dimensional existence, of an inward bearing of the burden and of an outward observation and obedience.

34

The teacher must set the example of obedience and observation. This is almost the opposite of being a taskmaster. The taskmaster watches how the task imposed gets done, and makes sure that it does get done. The pupil is told to write his essay, is rewarded for writing it, punished for not writing it. Obedience is exacted. Then the product is criticized. "Look how you did this, how you did that. Observe my way of doing it. Now observe Lamb, Bacon, Emerson." Observation of externals, of mere appearances, is encouraged. This is the standard approach. The pupil looms large. His performance is at stake. How does he function? There are ways of doing things. The conventions are observed, tradition is obeyed. At the same time the teacher does not know that all he is doing is furthering a fashion. Continually and repeatedly he mistakes a fashion for truth and presents it as reality. The pupil's unwillingness is castigated and becomes bad. The nonsense of the pupil is driven out of him and hardens. The curriculum becomes onerous to him, he is bored. But the opposite is not to be preferred. The pupil now demonstrates an aptitude for the work and writes essays that sparkle. Such diligence! Such industry! Good girl, well done. "Natasha gives me no trouble at all. She is bright, helpful, attentive. Does splendid work.

50

Quick to anticipate the teacher's wishes. Laughs at my jokes."
The curriculum in this case is absorbed. There is lucidity and
compliance. The teacher rewards this, praises the pupil in
front of the rest. 'Those twin impostors / failure and success,'
are not identified by her. She knows nothing of creative education. Real observation and obedience are tasks in themselves, where education is attempted. One continually and
repeatedly has to buckle down to something. It wells up inside and demands attention but we don't really get down to it.
It feels too much like work. A simple annoyance – why, here,
express it. You have a perfectly legitimate grievance. Or
there, a bit of pleasure. Let it out. Indulge yourself. Live a
little. You have a self, don't you? You are an individual? Do
you not have your rights? Hang the consequences. You are
only doing what everybody else is doing. – and why should I
not enjoy teaching? I come alive in the classroom. No need to
take everything to heart. I have a captive audience, by law.
Some performers have to work for that. And I get paid. Of
course you have to take some of the rough with the smooth.
True, I am an expert in my field and if they don't want to accept what I have to say to them, too bad. But I mean the pa-
per work, the eternal forms to fill out, the marking, and all
those meetings! Never mind. As soon as I step into that classroom my psyche dances. I am an actor. A bit of a clown. And
I like the bit of power that comes with the job. Let's face it,
now and again once does have a visible effect. And it's a
pleasure to exert one's will at times, when all else fails.

The creative teacher is familiar with all that. He also knows
what it is like to be totally frustrated and defeated. Such despair as can overcome a grownup among a group of pupils
within the context of an education system! Especially after
everything has gone well for a while. There seems to be total
obstruction. Worse, there is intentional interference. Strength
fails. Authority goes out the window. How can children be so

intrusive, so totally lacking in respect! They force me to behave like a nag, like a tyrant, and my nerves won't stand up to it. Sometimes I feel like a motherless child myself; I burst out crying. They are so much like monsters that the difference is negligible. But I know it's my own fault. I just don't measure up.

The creative teacher is familiar with the see-saw, the ups and the downs and the mood swings, the being pleased and the being disappointed, and – he uses them. They are, for him, his raw materials, even his tools and instruments. His good feelings and his bad feelings he equally – applies. He only has to notice them, and he steers them towards his work. They have less to do with him personally than with his field of operation. And it makes such a difference, when you know that a thorough frustration or a pure elation is potential for the good. Nothing else counts so much for sheer human meaning and worth, for individual security and personal freedom, than the confidence and knowledge that one has these two reins in one's hands. Frustration and elation. High spirits and despair. Disappointment and gratification. In themselves they are nothing; neither here nor there.

35

Again we notice the same fundamental educational pattern. The child is to learn something. The adult takes it upon herself to even the path for the child. Or: The teacher's presence brings about the difference between pupil and true child. The teacher appeals to the child and the pupil demonstrates what it is that gets in the way of the child's growth. The teacher takes this upon herself and continues to appeal to the child. She takes it upon herself as an adult, and as a mature, grownup person. This supplies the child with the example that is needed.

The adult confronts the child as a teacher but continues to be a mature human being. This is worth saying, because many a would-be teacher becomes a specialist and functions mechanically, so that very little, if anything, of the human being is left.

The duality of human being and teacher does not exist in standard education, where someone becomes one or the other. In the classroom the standard teacher is not aware of himself as a human being. He is playing a role. He may know that he is playing it, or he may forget after a while; in either case he is like an actor, who stops being an ordinary person as he steps on the stage, i.e. into the classroom. Children are often fascinated by standard teachers, who play their role imaginatively. They are intrigued by the performance of this actor and they are willing to participate in the play as an audience who now and again steps on the stage. These children become entirely pupils, in the classroom, and we can think of them as standard pupils; the teacher similarly becomes entirely teacher, but standard too.

Role playing goes on in the standard classroom. There is the pupil role and the teacher role. This aspect of standard education has perhaps never been sympathetically looked at. This is not possible except in comparison to creative education, where no such role playing goes on.

Standard education, as we know, has to do with survival, and this role playing, which is also a kind of pretending, and sort of a game, has for its effect that the attention of children is drawn to their ability to compromise with others and with the world, an this would be a fine thing if it were undertaken and presented in perspective, and as a useful survival skill in view of the primary life skill. What happens in actuality however is that these secondary skills are approached and learned as though there were not life skills, and consequently they become what we called 'survival tricks'. Compromise then becomes both a way of existence and a bad word. In reality, if we really wish to live and not just to survive, we do well to compromise in all sorts of areas, because then the way is smoothed that leads to real integrity and character.

Because something new is on the way, to which we cannot close our eyes with impunity, the difference between standard and creative education is blatantly obvious all around us, and only in theory can we speak of a standard approach that serves and supports the creative one. In theory we can describe how we would like things to be. But when we look round we cannot fail to notice that popular education is not working. One might even decide that it is 'not working any more', which is a slightly different observation.

We approach a diagnosis of this problem if we attribute the existence of it to the fact that 'the new' is not, in terms of popular education, recognized. It is neither acknowledged nor confronted. There is a blindness not only to the truth, but more specifically to the continual influence of the truth. This influence is not lessened if we ignore it. Ignorance does not put it way. A malaise sets in.

36

Today popular education everywhere is affected by this malaise. But this does not mean that once it was alright and now it has deteriorated. What it means is that the fault of its very inception now appears and becomes evident, where previously it was hidden. So, when we look at popular education today, we might feel like simply getting rid of it. Some liberal thinkers openly state their sympathy with such a move. They do not promise that the change would be painless, on the contrary, but they cannot see how we can come to terms with an honourable approach until we remove the lie.

There are those who maintain that popular education in the beginning, whenever that was, indeed aimed only at improved survival. We might see the start of popular education at the time when it was made civic law that all children had to go to school; such a law came into being in various countries as compulsory state education. The rulers of the population strive to get things in hand and under control. Due to a similar impulse a census is taken. See it as a civil service exercise. Popular education honestly seen as a civil service exercise, so as to get children off the streets and accustomed to regular habits, for example, is something rather different from education as a means to true, human maturity.

There is really no need to take issue with popular education except on political grounds, if, as some liberal philosophers suggest, the rights of children are being infringed upon. On grounds of education there is no issue, because real education begins from different premises. Once I know that human beings need to grow up and need help from mature adults to do so, and if I see human beings as unique, in the sense of having to traverse two states, and not only one, like all other beings, then I can just ignore popular education and concentrate on – creative education. That works if I write a doctrine on creative education, in order to gain understanding and so as to acquire a taste for it. But when a parent sees that his child is exposed to standard popular education for six or more hours a day he cannot help wondering what time might be left for anything else. Consequently, and understandably, he looks for loopholes in the system. Alternatives are tried.

The distinction I make between standard and creative education does not directly have any bearing on popular education at all. Only indirectly might it be pointed out that popular education is to a great extent now standard education. Certainly it would be nonsensical to try to make popular education creative, or even somewhat creative.

37

Education according to a standard can be supplied by anyone who is willing to limit himself to external and internal being. For example if I want to become more proficient in the way I get on with people I can go to someone with experience

55

aplenty and he can instruct me. It is not quite like carpentry or cookery because people have a way of parading their opinions and we try to fit in with them. But it is not creative either, because I am not willing to be changed. The way I behave is to change, but I myself am to remain the same.

The creative teacher is willing to be changed. She observes without interfering. External and internal reality is what she observes. Her teaching has nothing to do with these. She intends to guide the true child in a way that will guard him against any such interference. What do we mean by this observed reality? The creative teacher instinctively knows. It is something that comes about during the creative education process. The true child is now taking an interest. The first attempts are made at communication, and these we can call self-expression. The pupil comes up with all sorts of notions of his own, which he himself barely recognizes. Certainly he does not understand them and has no notion of what they mean. The true child speak through the pupil: we do well to acquaint ourselves with this phenomenon. The human being is beginning to become creative. The teacher continues to view this young human being as true child and pupil. As teacher she relates to the pupil, as guide she relates to the true child.

38

Internal and external reality – real alright, but to be observed. Instinctively the teacher knows. That something like this should come to pass is a sure sign of progress for the guide. It is as if all those forces which were ranged against the child's true expression of itself showed their hand. So this is a forceful reality, but internally and externally observable. And the observation makes it safe. The true child trust itself out into this reality because he senses (we could legitimately sa: 'it senses', because gender as yet does not play a role) – how the teacher makes his environment safe. The guide stands between the new child and unreal forces. We can

56

speak of the <u>new</u> child now, as soon as expression has begun to take place. If the teacher did not observe, the forces would endanger the child and it would once again decline.

Just as the teacher at the start had to combat false influences so that the true child might come forth, so the guide now combats old forces for the sake of the new child. Mortification was what we called the effect of those falsehoods that kept the true child in bondage. In the case of the new child we can speak of a handicap. The new child would be more or less handicapped if it lost its guide, and if the old forces were at this crucial time not made safe by him – were not observed.

However just as the child can be cured of any mortification, so can any handicap be undone. When the teacher detects a handicap, he knows that the new child has been thwarted in its self-expression, so she creates an especially safe environment for the child. This special safety is once again inward work for the teacher and we intend to describe it.

39

But first we have to get more of a feel, more of a sense – of what this is which the child would experience to its detriment if it were not observed, and which, if and while it is observed, provides something like the practice area and testing ground for the new child. We have it at our fingertips right here and now, at this stage in our doctrine. It threatens at every moment to overcome us like a bleak moodiness, like a persuasion of personal worthlessness, of individual ineffectiveness. It feels like nothing can be done so why bother.

The central experience here is of mood, which is, by the way, the essence of religion. A clean and clear mood gives personal satisfaction, but where this sobriety does not exist, our own existence is upset; we are in a bad mood, in a vile, an evil mood. And if we are in a 'good' mood, we have to be careful. Oh, the ambiguity of a good mood! So much that 'feels good' is in fact inhuman. Let us above all keep in mind the need for sobriety. We have tested this ourselves. Our own beginnings were self-expressive, just as the 'new child' in the pupil is self-expressive, and we have had to learn how to renounce our self, instead of developing a self. This sounds paradoxical, but observe what happens. Continue to observe, as the moods flicker, and as you flounder. Mood swings are merely invitations to observe, and symptoms of a lack of sober observation.

The self-expression is an excellent thing, but only in terms of what it, in itself, means, and what comes afterwards, not because of any product of it. In other words, there must be self-expression before we have a self to renounce, so as to be able to follow our guide. I am putting us, as students of this doctrine, into the position of the new child. This new child is extremely vulnerable and at the same time 'full of itself'. Take a look at the Euphorion figure in Goethe's Faust. The parents are puzzled fearful, near despair over the 'mood swings' of their charge. "Brief joys must be our lot / by woes overwhelmed."

The singular plight of many teenagers nowadays springs from an inability to deal with moods. The self has come into being but self-expression is thwarted, so that renunciation of self cannot even be properly envisioned. The teacher as guide looks out for the first signs of self-expression in his pupil and then observes very closely. "Out with the old, in with the new!" she says. She neither encourages nor discourages self-expression. She does not wish to give the pupil a notion that what is being expressed is of value, but she transmits her gladness about the fact that self-expression goes on. No wonder we say that the guide must be wise. She has an instinctive perception of what, to the untrained eye, would appear as mere selfishness.

And, indeed, the way the 'new child' initially manifests itself cannot help but be selfish, that is to say: self-oriented and self-determined. Provocative visions of the world are produced. These are eternal. There is self-interest combined with surprise ad discovery, and of course with anger at not being immediately 'believed'. This goes on internally.

Historically, 'society' separates itself self-consciously from this sort of 'individualism', which then takes refuge in artistry, which in turn then strives, simultaneously, to subvert that society and to 'live off' it. Within every artist (not art worker) we see the thwarted new child and the relative lack of self-renunciation. With our doctrine of creative education we manage to become much more aware of the initial requirements of the 'new child', of the environment that comes into being so specifically all around it, all due to this necessary self-expression, all of which is to be wisely observed by the teacher as guide.

40

The teacher observes what goes on, as the pupil 'comes out of himself'. She knows how important this active observation is, on her part. It is a service. She renders the new child the service of allowing it to come to terms with its own existence here, and with its discovery of itself. Of course she aims at a smooth transition. She does not want the new child to get stuck in self-expression either. This is to be a transitional phase, but an important one, and just long enough for the child to acquire this skill of observation from the teacher.

To be stuck in <u>self-expression</u> is the same a to become addicted to <u>self-consciousness</u>. Observation of its 'new' environment serves the child in a direction away from self-consciousness.

We can see self-expression and self-consciousness as the two sides of the new child, each giving rise to its own hemisphere, self-expression externally and self-consciousness internally.

We cannot emphasize enough how crucially important it is for every human being to go through this stage of development, and what a great difference it makes if the human being is guided through this stage – and guided it must be – at the organically opportune time, rather than being handicapped. There is no question of a teacher doing anything too early. Neglect and misconception is the great risk, once the first signs of new human being are beginning to show up. An unwise teacher thinks, then, only of misbehaviour, and she condemns. And certainly if several pupils arrive at this stage of development at the same time, things can get difficult and special measures may have to be taken. The pupil who misbehaves must be brought back to an awareness of himself as a true child, as a new human being, which calls for true discipline. The unwise teacher, who is not a guide, sees only misbehaviour and knows nothing of the underlying 'good new', so all she can do is condemn. The wise guide understands all this misbehaviour and approaches it as a sign of something good. Whatever constraints she applies are not harsh but all the more effective for being firm and kindly.

The true nature of discipline, even of discipleship, can be conned in this context.

41

Let us stay with this 'transitional sphere' for the time being.

What the guide observes is self-expression and self-consciousness. He is eager that there should occur as little handicap as possible. He knows that handicap sets in if the child does not learn to observe. Then self-consciousness becomes intemperate and self-consciousness strained.

One might legitimately ask: How does the teacher know when the time is ripe to bring certain influences to bear so as to prevent handicap? After all, self-consciousness and self-expression must go on for a while so that the child may begin to learn to observe. But the point is, that the teacher cannot know the time. She has no business concerning herself with the inside or the outside clock of growth. Her particular and fully occupational task is to notice self-expression and self-consciousness as early as possible and then to observe. If we have trouble with this, we probably need to update our understanding of the meaning of observation. It has nothing to do with the scientist's attempt to observe so 'objectively' that what he observes remains the same as though he were not observing it. The observation we mean is like a service, and it does the child good.

It brings to bear on the child's new liveliness an influence of care.

And where handicap has set in, that is to say: where self-expression is strained and self-consciousness intemperate, a special observation is called for.

42

Let us call this special observation careful. The state of youthful existence nowadays is such that this special 'careful' observation is mandatory. There is, in other words, a high dgee of handicap. And please keep in mind that an actual handicap presupposes, after all, that new life is available. Where self-expression and self-consciousness have not even come into being, no handicap exists; but nothing else exists either.

So the teacher who carefully observes a handicapped child does so gladly, because he knows there is something to observe. The pupil who has not yet responded to the intervention of the teacher cannot be of interest to the guide. The handicapped child is of great interest to the guide.

We repeat: There is handicap of the soul, the mind and body, the spirit and the flesh. And handicap is not of being but of function.

Once again the guide experiences the child's handicap as his own. His own functioning is curtailed but he knows that the handicap in the child is of such functions as pertain not to free behaviour but to self-expression and self-consciousness. So the transferred handicap is not of the teacher's free action either, of his function as a carefully observing guide, but it will seem to the teacher that his own self-expression and self-consciousness is strained and intemperate. Until then he was neither self-conscious nor expressing his self, but suddenly he senses that intemperate self-consciousness and that strained self-expression in himself. Let us just say he experiences <u>intemperance</u> and <u>strain</u>.

A standard teacher, an inexperienced guide, or simply an unwise person, would mistake this intemperance and strain for his own and he would either react or control. He would either blame the pupils and correct them or blame himself and control himself. From the way we have traced the origins of these experiences we can see how misguided and wasteful this is. The true guide, when he knows this experience of intemperance and strain, realizes that now his work as special guide can begin. He does not become self-expressive or self-conscious – and the tendency to do so exists in him too, of course – but he begins to observe very carefully. If he flies off the handle after all, well, he can apologize, and better luck next time. If he goes into a mood, good or bad, self-consciously, he will probably get a sharp reminder to bring him back to his creativity and he will know that mishaps like this happen. In other words he wastes no time deploring his failures but as soon as possible returns to careful observation – which lets him come to terms with any further intemperance or strain.

The only real evidence a creative teacher has of handicap in a pupil is the strain and intemperance he experiences in himself. Immediately he knows of the true child in conflict.

As a teacher becomes a better guide, the gap between intemperance/strain painfully experienced and joyful recognition of the existence of a true child, of new life, implied by this, narrows. There are fewer incidents of experienced intemperance actually turning into self-consciousness; of experienced strain turning into self-expression as the guide improves.

Let us take a closer look at this careful observation with which the guide confronts the intemperance and the strain that have been transferred to him. There is no question of meddling with them, analytically or otherwise. The main concession to make here is that judgment does not come into it. Instead of judgment, which leads to conclusions, what we strive for here is understanding, so that, instead of making more of ourselves, in reaction to strain and intemperance projected onto the pupils, we make less of ourselves, making at the same time less of these transferred handicaps. Our ambition, as guides, is, after all, to undo the handicaps, and we can do that right away. It is not a true observation, and certainly not a careful one, that is exercised judgmentally. I, as a teaching guide, am mature and have nothing to fear from the handicaps displayed by my pupil. I am therefore not on my guard, not in a defensive position. A standard teacher, by comparison, must insist on his superior role, which he calls his authority, which is of course delegated, not native. It can be withdrawn from him at a moment's notice, this delegated authority. My own authority resides in my being a mature human being. It cannot be taken from me. I might lose it, by becoming immature, due to immature behaviour, and then of course this authority diminishes in proportion, but then again this immature trend can be reversed by me, as I submit to a higher, native authority. This difference between delegated and native authority characterizes the distinction of creative and standard education, by the way. We will come back to that. Right now we can just make amends for our own immaturity by demonstrating an example of unjudgmental observation.

One way of coming to the point here might be to emphasize that the guide does not make observations, he observes. He takes note of that which is to be observed, recognizing it for what it is, and then keeps his eye on it as he understands the true child whose faculties are handicapped. His observation embraces the handicap along with the child. It begins with the strain and the intemperance and stays with these until they are quite distinct, until there is no more danger, in the guide, of a tendency to self-expression on account of the intemperance or of an inclination to self-consciousness because of the strain – and then the true child is observed too, as a functioning person.

We might also say that the guide atones for the handicaps of the child. He makes up, or compensates for them. It may help him if he forgives the strain and the intemperance. He certainly has the native authority to do so. Where he associates atonement and forgiveness with his task of observation he is even less likely to become judgmental, to wish to control and classify, to lord it over the pupil.

43

Remember that the handicap is of such function as we described as self-expression and self-consciousness of the true child. One might assume now that, with the handicap removed or undone by the observing guide, the child is free to continue with those two germinal functions. However, self-expression and self-consciousness can never be free. What does happen is that the child now begins to observe on his own account. (At this stage, by the way, gender begins to assert itself.) Consciousness and expression are consequently not anymore of the self. This is a major step forward. The child has learned something, and this is the first thing the child has learned. He imitates, in the truest sense of the word, the observation, the observing activity of the guide. Observation now becomes functional for the child and the self is eclipsed. Expression and consciousness become observational, or observant, rather than 'selfish'.

44

On the surface it seems incongruous that a person should enter a classroom, join the company of several youngsters and then, at one and the same time, instruct them in the skills of writing, for instance, and teach them how to observe. What, we feel bound to ask, can the formation of letters, the spelling of words and the construction of sentences have in common with the discovery of the new child, with strained self-expression and untempered self-consciousness and with careful observation? Do we seriously expect that a teacher should be able to divide his attention so thoroughly? The elements of outward occupation are to be at his fingertips, and in fact, in an outward fashion, not as externals, while the inward development of these young human beings remains ever present to him, constituting the focal point of his interest.

But we demand no more of the teacher than we do of ourselves as mature, growing human beings. We are aware of our inward development, individual for each one of us, and we pay attention to outward effect and influence. We know that our inward health and strength demands prior attention, but then we take pains with our personal relationships and we continually arrange matters outwardly in compliance with our knowledge and understanding, so that our individual discoveries become communally useful. The experience of one is of benefit for many.

So how is our own relationship with one another different from the teacher/pupil relationship? Or how is it different from a parent/child relationship?

When you and I as adults are in communication, we certainly make allowances for one another's immaturities, and our goal is life and a greater abundance of life. We know that we need to approach inwardly, and that external reality can be made to serve this inward acquaintance. You enter my house. You bring a gift. I express gratitude in terms of time-honoured conventional phrases. I observe as many of those conventions as possible because I want to make you comfortable. I bring out the best chair for you, offer you food and drink, while you do your best to put me, the host, at my ease. You praise the décor of my house, you show me how pleased you are with my attentions – and gradually a transition takes place. Eternals have served their purpose, we have served one another, now we engage inwardly. Talk comes around, from common interests, to individual concerns. 'Confession' takes place. One of us suddenly has something new to say, has made a discovery and decides, upon reflection, to speak. As talk moves to speech, externals are nearly forgotten – not to mention 'internals' such as your comfort in my house and my satisfaction with having done what I can as your host. The host/guest relation becomes personal and individual, both, as we strive to be of one mind, as we allow our souls to be re-freshed and as we invoke our spirit in the interest of one an-other. As we love one another, each one overcomes, in him-self, the experienced shortcomings and transgressions of the other, all for the sake of progress understood as an abundance of life.

We began as host and guest, we part as friends. We have both been enriched. Our inward work has taken shape, out-wardly. We are more fit to deal with the next problem, we have greater resources for the benefit of others who come our way. 'Inward' and 'outward' are seen, are known, to be one by us, and this is such valuable knowledge, indispensable for the success of every piece of work we undertake, in personal relationship or otherwise. When next time we come across external and internal data, we know that this is a semblance

66

of reality and we are to make it serve. And when the inward/outward division is upon us, we understand this as the approach of reality, with which we join and engage. And then we 'worship' in reality itself and reach a conclusion. – this is normal behaviour for adults, who value their maturity and admit their immaturity. Next time you can invite me to your own house, and then we begin again, prudently, as host and guest, precisely in the interest and hope of the renewed friendship. Only an idealist will always want to begin as a friend – and get nowhere, while the realist 'pretends to know' that true friendship is impossible. But you and I would really be friends, and that is a worthwhile and creative work.

Compare to this now the parent/child relationship.

Here the maturity of an adult is not confronted by immaturity, since immaturity pertains to adults, but by youth, which accounts for a slightly different relationship, but still externals and internals are made to serve by the adult, while the child leaves him- or herself in the hands of the adult and gradually learns to differentiate between his own inner being and everything else, which is ordered by the adult and rendered meaningful. This is how it is, if all goes well. The parental activity of the adult is comprised of this meaningful ordering of the child's world. Meanwhile the child's inner being, all that he discovers as his sensibilities, his moods and dispositions, over which he as yet has neither control nor mastery, develops and becomes more noticeable, more present, to the child. <u>The parent creates circumstances.</u> He does not intervene, like the teacher, and he does not engage with an inward awareness of the child, as with a friend, because such an awareness does not yet exist. We can say that the child grows up as he interacts with the parentally created circumstances, and as that meaningful order becomes inwardly more and more accessible to him.

As mature adults we are not put off by our own inconveniences, by what bothers us about ourselves, about one another and the world. This serves to distinguish us from children, who need a mature adult to whom they can relate so that their discomforts and diseases do not get the better of them. An adult can say to himself: "I don't the least bit feel like doing such and such, but I am going go do it all the same because my intelligence serves me better than any feelings. My intelligence is my contact with that which is great, true and complete. Consequently I want to make use of that contact especially at such times as when I feel disinclined to do anything at all. I must not wait to be prompted before I act. And the most dangerous prompt, perhaps, is that feeling of energy that sweeps us off our feet and mixes us actively up in affairs before we have taken time to take stock. Much safer to act when first a disinclination is to be overcome.

And such action impresses a child immensely. It demonstrates authority. And a child desires authority without being able to say precisely how or why. Children wish they could make up their own minds, especially where external and internal promptings are lacking. The teacher who sets out to introduce his pupil to some aspect of the world does well, therefore, to keep in mind the child's longing for authority, and, of course, for the personal freedom that comes with it. If the subject matter is presented with authority, the child grows; if not, the pupil is weighed down. What does authority mean to us? Delegated authority is second-best. Children are taken in by it if native authority is absent.

Native authority, strangely enough, begins as soon as we strive to be honest and truthful. Uniquely, it links our being and our doing, our existence and our function. Neither of these alone can cause anything to come about. But this is precisely how we ought to view authority. He who has it can 'make things happen'. In comparison, the one who only is and does nothing is perpetually overlooked, while he who only does and is nothing perpetually misses the point.

Now it is very easy to fall into the one or the other of these two. It is like falling into the water and falling into the fire. Rarely do we notice right away when something like this goes wrong, because of the pleasure that attaches to it. Senseless activity is a pleasure because we forget our self and feel energetic. This is like the intemperate self-expression of the child, and in the case of adults we refer to it as immaturity. Idle dreaming is the other side of it, and this is a protraction of the child's strained self-consciousness. Hamlet's is the typical problem of the adult who cannot for the life of him come up with any authority. As an idle dreamer he begins to 'see ghosts' which lure him even further into self-consciousness, until the ghost frightens him into mere activity, and then he makes a mess of things.

The problem of authority is so basically human that we should take it to heart. It comes to light as a problem not while we limit ourselves to delegated authority, but as soon as we realize that we ourselves should have native authority, and that there is no excuse for being without it.

Where we miss it, there it is possible. Those of us who feel they ought to have it, do have it, but not sufficiently formed. Those who are perfectly content with delegated authority, whether they exercise it or obey it, have no native authority.

We call it native authority because we are born with it – and then something happens. We become dishonest and untruthful and this native authority goes out the window or falls by the way.

In children this authority has to be developed and we do well to bring this development, in our thinking and feeling, in line with honesty and truthfulness. In other words, if we would develop the authority in our children we must teach them how to be honest and truthful.

It is not easy to be honest. There is more to it than many of us probably suppose. The same goes for truthfulness. something within us wants out into the light of day, and if we don't facilitate that, we are not honest but dishonest; if we actually prevent it we are untruthful and false. There is something in us that definitely wants out into the light of day. Some of us are anxious to find out what it is, so that they can make the path straight for it, as the saying goes, but I dare say most people couldn't care less. They define honesty and truthfulness to suit themselves.

Those of us who want to find out what it is that wants out, so that they can facilitate it, will never find out, because they have the cart before the horse. All we need to know and all we can initially know is that within us something, call it spirit, seeks to manifest itself. We cannot find out what in particular it is until we have in fact prepared for it. We can talk, and write, about this preparation in detail. Spirit, however, will not make its home in us until we have sufficiently prepared. Authority, now, can be defined as an availability or readiness of spirit.

Not all spirit is good. This seems to be a terribly difficult lesson to learn today, probably because we have become so dispirited, so dishonest and false, that suddenly we say: any spirit is better than none.

Interestingly enough, the origin of life is spirit. That which is in us and wants to come into the light of day is spirit, but as soon as it does come out we call it life. So we see how crucially honesty and truthfulness are connected with life itself.

By being honest and truthful we make it possible for the spirit within us to become life. It becomes the life which we then have, because we give it out. The particular shape that this life takes is, again, not initially up to us. Only much later, when we have some authoritative creation experience and practice in giving our life can we shape life itself. Therein lies greatness and mastery.

<h2 style="text-align:center">46</h2>

If we have some purpose in our work as teachers, it will aggravate us to see individual authority stamped out. One sits in the world with one's spirit intact but no one to talk to. The lazy hankering after delegated authority fills the air. Meanwhile the spirit in each one of us strives for recognition. We need to be educated away from incumbent slavishness. What happens everywhere instead is that obedience to tricks is drummed into our children. The survival tricks of the age are the last bastion of a popular morality, where a false spirit pretends to be great.

Energy is applauded, in any and every form. This is a polemic now, so I make no attempt to be accurate. Spirit is honoured, in any and every form, shape or size. What makes us so nervous? Surely not merely the lack of a cosmic mythology! What about that all-embracing fear of being ploughed under? We suspect that unless we participate in the spirit of the age our pain will be endless. But there is no such spirit of the age. We can shout ourselves hoarse for it, it won't come. Something else is afoot. We will not be swept off our feet by an epoch-making cultural movement. Any such movements that stir us today are false and dishonest. They derive from a spirit that has not been properly stamped and earmarked yet. The spirit of dishonesty and falsehood flaps its wings and descends with a mighty rush, hopefully to take us by surprise by producing great wonders.

Our present task as educators is to unmask this spirit. If it should happen that future appearances are foretold and the frontiers of space are made void, we must ask: To what end? And yet it would make sense, would it not, if we are to be bamboozled, that time and space itself should be 'liberated' and made lawless?

Those who are tied to the limitations of time and space are nowhere near in the same boat with those who respect and honour those limitations because they understand their creative purpose.

We return here to the role that 'externals' and 'internals' play in our lives, and what they mean to us, what use we make of them and how, if at all, we depend on them.

47

The spirit in each one of us strives for recognition, and we owe it to one another as communal beings to render the service that allows this spirit to become life. However, only good spirit is willing to live. Bad and evil spirits also seek embodiment and frequently find it.

Now the educator must make honesty and truthfulness his watchwords so that good spirit will gain entry into the light of day. Aspects of the world which he introduces to those to be educated are initially externals and internals, so that when a pupil first comes into contact with something new here it will indeed be new to him in appearance but not in substance, since all that makes up the world originates as human nature, even as human beings do. All that is created or made, including ourselves to a certain extent, has humanity as its essence, so that when we look at a pine tree honestly and truthfully we see another appearance of something that exists previously in us. By previously I mean that our looking at that tree honestly and truthfully brings about an experience of recognition so that we can say: "There too am I."

And so with all aspects of the world, whether visible or invisible – as we get to know them, learning them, so to speak – we discover what we have in common with them.

We must keep in mind that there is an infinite number of aspects to the world, so that by 'world' we do not accidentally mean something that has to do exclusively with time and space. However, the fact that time and space allow us to approach the world, in an infinite number of ways, this is something for which we have cause to be grateful. There are those who would do away with time and space, so as to see the world more really, or truly, or deeply, but in this they are misguided. Precisely by that spirit of falsehood and dishonesty which always seeks the back door by which to enter the house of creation, so naturally what happens as an outcome of this is a plurality of worlds and a time that is endless. There are also those who would exhaust the world in terms of time and space, so that each would swear by his own aspect, and this must be interrupted by apocalypse and catastrophe.

So we are grateful for time and space, and glad that we are able to approach the world in terms of them, for the sake of our enrichment, since we and the world amount to more than can be explained or known in terms of time and space.

48

So much for the educator's attitude towards the world. He sees it creatively, in that he desires to bring to it the good spirit-life that may come forth from those he educates. He sees the world as something that deserves to be honoured, not as a crisis called 'this world' and studied sceptically, represented ironically, finally to be given up.

The educator's world, to which he educates, is not something that serves him, during the influence of a desired effect on his charges, but he learns to serve it. His is evidently a world different from the one that morally ensnares and spiritually enslaves. It is such a world as lives and breathes in the works of Albert Schweitzer, for example, for whom time and space was ever the format for real education, honestly and truthfully pursued.

The normal attitude, towards the world, of a man with courage and authority, allows him to take it as it comes. He would rather tamper with his attitude than with the world, if something goes awry. He knows that as he perceives, so it turns out for him. He does not suffer from the parasite's epistemology, where nothing is ever quite right because the times are wrong and the place is wrong.

The educator takes it upon himself to demonstrate that the time and place is always right. But in order to be able to know that this is so he must be a creative person in his own right, otherwise he would only be repeating gossip. Nobody believes and accepts that the here and now is the best we have except from someone with authority. This native authority the creative educator maintains for himself by keeping vital his attitude towards the world – towards world – as an infinite number of aspects all equally justifiable, not as mirrors in which we see ourselves flattened and reversed, but as points of human recognition, so that we once again may say: "There too am I", or "There too are we.".

49

We cannot make ourselves live in a world that has no interest for others. However we must choose among that which interests us, and select for some purpose, with some end in mind. We ourselves want to be educated, which is why we subordinate ourselves to creative human beings in our vicinity. The way they behave in our presence is dear to us, whether we have them in the flesh or in books. An artwork can educate us, if we know how to subordinate our faculties to the personal appeal of that work. A particular aspect of the world is 'measured to size', as it were, in every artwork, so that anyone who cares might excel in pursuit of what has been 'worked out'. This excellence is something that speaks to the educator's heart. He means it with any effort he makes.

To us who wish to be educated, excellence means the very next difficulty overcome. We have even been known to surround ourselves with difficulties so that excellence might serve. But our educator selects for us problems as he sees fit. He lives at a certain time, somewhere, and brings out of himself, creatively, articulate solutions to problems only dimly sensed. A part of our subordination, of our obedience even, stems from our trust that the problems he selects to solve and the difficulties he chooses to overcome, excellently, would have been ours, even if we cannot come right out and say they were. He exceeds and he excels, and in that we wish to join him. Not that he could do that if he did it for himself; he must do it for us, and of course he knows that. We in turn trust him. Often he speaks with a voice of concern for us about troubles we still have not recognized, and sometimes we cannot acknowledge such troubles until he voices his concern. Therein lies his god-given talent as an educator. On that account we respect him even if we cannot always plumb his motivations.

We can seriously even speak of such a thing as our belief in an educator. But here we take care, because nothing does damage like misguided belief. What if the man has our welfare at heart? Should we not make amends in our own hearts to suit him? How to be certain! Falsehood is taught as though it were the truth. A hectoring bully is unmasked and displays sincerity. Some are so eager to educate that one wonders at the nature of their reward. Others are simple souls, wedded to reproof, but gentle withal, and great perpetrators of a patience that functions in its own right.

So we need to come to terms with what it is we require. We who are adults of one sort or another, mature and immature, have no way of deciding how our minds should be tutored and our bodies trained in the interest of human growth, because that, by definition, lies beyond us as individuals. But we can come to terms in much detail and depth with our wish to be educated. The child, who <u>wants</u> to be educated, cannot do that. We ourselves, even with the least experience of maturity in our soul, are able to reflect on what it is we wish, and by doing that we not only meet the prospective educator halfway, but become able to tell the true from the false, the honest from the dishonest. If we genuinely take ourselves to task as to where we feel strain and in what we are intemperate – and this will still serve as a measure of our condition – then what we come up with, upon sufficient perseverance, is something we should never let fall into disrespect or disuse, and that is the organic faculty of common sense.

Why organic? Because based on nothing that serves us as a sign. The charlatan, the false prophet, the antichrist – good heavens, who knows what else – these too work in signs and great wonders. They foretell the future and stretch the past until it squeaks. The laws of space and time, they turn them upside down, to please us, to make our eyebrows rise. These miracle workers – what signs they produce! Because they know our weaknesses. To be fair, those are their own weaknesses, and they pander to them. Before they lie to us, they lie to themselves.

So we need something other than signs, to guide us through the welter of ego-advertisement, past the bog of miracle and magic. We need something better than proof by appearances. We need something quietly inserted between our intellect and emotion that is capable of receiving impressions from both.

Organic common sense is a topical achievement. We need to be perfectly honest and truthful with ourselves. And we must begin with our wish to be much more mature. While we remain indifferent to our various immaturities, obvious or covert, we have nothing to gain and the remainder of our maturity to lose.

Indifference, however, may, at a moment's notice, be turned into care. We need only inspect our reaction to words such as these. No sign is evoked on their behalf. They stand for nothing and they represent nothing. But what they are is real. It might occur to us to wonder how such an achievement

76

is managed. Question your wish to be educated and see for yourself.

50

Calculation brings us into contact with a truth of sorts, and even organic common sense begins with calculation. We count the cost. As we strive educationally towards more maturity, how can we all underwrite the same creed? First comes the question: To what am I suited, and what suits me. Not in the privacy of our mind do we ask, but while we experience some contact of the world. Mystic experience is not educational, but valid in its own right. Whatever way the world makes impression on our moods and senses, this is to show us ourselves as we are. It takes a while to learn the laws that shape us. First we admit, to ourselves, that indeed we are shaped. We stand four square in the wind of adversity – then love bowls us over. Our miserable few pence run out but we gain an eternal friend meanwhile. Or we suffer correction from pain and find that another, near to us, benefits from the agony.

There are types of character. Each, by definition, stands differently to the world. Each has a contact of its own to fulfil and we are not to argue with the way we are made. Our creature characteristics are the way they are for a reason up to us to discover. If we help ourselves now to the ways and means at our disposal, however modest and seemingly insignificant, we will be shown, in ourselves, by the world, what is needful. But we must be willing to begin small. The discovery of the world as a pristine reality is not vouchsafed the one who still hankers after some conquest of the world; he sees only a horrid shell he can never quite crack to get at the kernel. Neither does the one who has not yet conquered himself get a glimpse of it.

51

There is in the beginning of our experience of the world a distinct sense of wonder. Unless we have once at least known that wonder we are not very likely to know what the world is, but our senses are preoccupied with their own sweet memory. The fact that this sweetness cannot last does not bother us, until one day the zest goes out of what we thought life was and we have nothing to replace it.

Now we can, if we choose to do so, become alert to what ails us. Our world-weariness really has nothing to do with the world but everything with us. There are those who would tear us forcibly out of this weariness if we pay them money, but the absence of weariness is not the presence of the world, and what we desire, after all, is some vision of the world, of the pristine world – as I call it, so as to show that I don't mean that picture painted by our worn-out senses.

But is there such a thing as his pristine world, the experience of which begins as wonder?

If I teach you that there is, you may learn that there is. If I teach you the world that embraces the sum total of all your experience in a sense of wonder then you may believe what I say, because I know what I mean. I say nothing except what I know from experience. I tell you of the world that radiates with a light of its own. I call that light the light of day. Can you accept that? This is an education. Not that I want you to forget what you know so as to believe what I say. But you can experience what I have experienced and then you must let us all know what it was. Is that education, to relate what we know? Not quite. Certainly we must elate what we know, but in order to educate we must do something else, in addition. We must take the responsibility for having related what we know. Quite often we all just relate what we experienced, because that makes life much more interesting for several of us.

But if I tell you what I know and you turn the other way without making reply, or if you reply by telling me in turn what you know, then this is communication, but not yet education.

Not until you see in my knowledge something that satisfies your desire for real experience, such as an experience of the pristine world, and then you make that your own, overcoming meanwhile your world-weariness which would bid you remain defeated in complaint – not until then does education take place: because you yourself overcome an evil while reaching for a good.

You do not yet appropriate the good. That implies actual creativity. Education takes us to the point where we have a vision of the good, of the right, of the true and beautiful. And I repeat: We ourselves, as adults, must overcome the hindrance in ourselves that keeps the good from us, we cannot get anyone to do that for us. No teacher, no miracle worker, no messiah, can do us good in that way, because that would be magic, but magic is bogus and only pretends. There always have been magicians and sorcerers, though in every century they travel under a different banner, and their promise, usually for money, is that if we listen to them our hindrances and shortcomings and misgivings will melt away. They would 'educate' us by rooting out our evil for us. All they can give us is a respite from intelligence and a numbness where pain was.

52

So it takes someone with experience of the pristine world if adult education is to take place. And not only adult education. No one will believe what you say if you speak only from hearsay; if you merely repeat the words of another. And there is such a thing as experience of the pristine world. It begins with, and is circumscribed by, a sense of wonder. The work of poets is to make that experience palpable for others.

The work of educators is to present that experience to others and to abide with them while they overcome their own hindrances to such experience. Socrates according to Plato, presented himself explicitly as such an educator, first and foremost. He behaved responsibly. His experience was not of the pristine world but of something close to it.

Whatever aspect of the world we choose, the way we communicate it must inform somehow of the pristine world. As we begin to take an interest in the world, we naturally look at it from some point of view. And there is no number of such points of view. Every individual person has his own authentic point of view from which he may start, and no two authentic points of view are exactly the same. It seems absurd even to try to imagine such a thing. What we need to be reminded of, however, educationally, is that we definitely are endowed with such a capacity for our own authentic point of view vis-à-vis the world. Each one of us is born with authenticity. An educator knows that absolutely about himself. When he educates, he operates first and foremost from his own authentic point of view. He was born with the capacity for that and he was reborn to use it, to exercise that capacity. Again I use the word 'reborn', but in a sense entirely distinct from any religious sect or creed. To be reborn simply means to come into full possession of our human being, which being, while we are not yet in full possession of it – or to the degree that we are not yet in full possession of it – we call our human nature.

We sense that we might have an authentic point of view long before we actually communicate anything from that point of view. That which sets us back, if we are not careful, is whatever is presented to us from an inauthentic point of view. People who preach to us dishonestly and untruthfully, and people who reject us unless we agree to adopt their own point of view, can easily be tolerated, however, and then we will not suffer setbacks.

Let me say it again: In order to come into the possession of our own, singular mode of perception, from which to start, so that we can become conversant with a variety of such modes, we must ourselves overcome or do away with, or annihilate, what it is that prevents such perception. These are natural hindrances. They are not caused by ourselves or by others. Some would create their own hindrances, so that they can overcome them in a perfectly controlled fashion, but we can see the dishonestly in that. Others create hindrances for us so that they can then overcome them for us, usually for money, but we can see the untruthfulness in that. Nowadays it is always important to take infinite care, because so many educators vie for our attention so that we will add to their glory or to their purse.

53

An educator knows how important for himself is his own way of looking at things, so no wonder that this is the first faculty he encourages in others. "You must learn to use the eyes and ears you were born with. You must learn to use the voice, the mode of expression you were born with. You must learn to think and feel the way you were born to think and feel. Only in that can all your subsequent faculties be rooted. If you try to adopt the prevalent and conventional point of view, the fashionable vision of the times, you die. I assume you would prefer to live. Some of you may have to lay aside a great number of opinions and beliefs, to unlearn them, in a sense, so as to discover your individual vision and imagination. You will have to do that yourselves, no one can do it for you. You must show by your actions that you are willing to return to your original stature, quite irrespective of what you seem to have become in the meantime, with or without the help or hindrance of others. Unless you demonstrate this willingness, your original vision will not work. Your original stature may seem to you, from our present perspective, shamefully insignificant, horribly vulnerable, but to it you must return, not because anyone pushes you there but because you see the sense in doing so yourself. And you must never suppose that you can see the world clearly except through your own original eyes. From here it must begin; from your perception of the world."

This is the educator's ambition, then, that authentic vision should become possible for others, and to that end he exerts himself.

Wisely he sets out by telling us what he sees, what he thinks, feels and knows. His perception of the world is entirely his own and he demonstrates this. He gives us numerous examples of what it means, in his case, to have genuine experience of the world.

If right now we are not capable of authentic perception, of knowing as only we in the singular and no one else can, then we will not be able to make sense of this educator's testimony. If we are accustomed, perhaps even addicted, to the conventional and fashionable point of view, an original thought or observation will seem to us impenetrable, not because of what the educator is talking about, but on account of what he is saying. He might be describing a walk along the hedgerow, which is an ordinary enough walk to take, but how he describes it will completely go past us and we will not have the benefit of any of his authentic human nature or genuine personality. It is as if he were speaking a language unknown to us.

And of course he is very well aware of our predicament. A communication gap has opened between him and us, and this is nothing unexpected for him. He fully realizes it could not be otherwise.

54

This communication gap bothers us, like a tension in our make-up. We feel dissatisfied with the way things are going and while we do not exactly blame ourselves for our incomprehension, we do all the same feel urged to do something about it. Something about the educator attracts us. He expresses it, in his manner, in his gestures and behaviour – in the way he approaches us and presents himself to us. It is almost as if he would be willing to concern himself with us whether we accept his message or not, and, perhaps even more important, whether we accept him in person or not.

Communication can be seen as an exchange of personality, so that you and I, while we communicate, rise out of our individuality and become personal. The educator seems to have developed the singular skill in himself of rising to his own personality even while we remain stuck, for the time being, in our individuality. In this we appreciate his creativity. While we remain outwardly glum and taciturn, because we just do not seem capable of any better at the moment, he cheerful proceeds with his expression of himself according to his own authentic point of view. He may talk about the weather, about the mysteries of plant growth, about the development of a variety of number systems out of different attitudes, by people, to their physical environment – but what he is really saying, and what we cannot, so far, assimilate, because he cannot other than say it from his singular vantage point as a creative person, is: "The world is a marvel and life is worth living. Look how intricately all appearances are combined and connected! Only imagine the joy to be experienced in a world of such vital magnitude! Even the elements suffer gain and loss, as though in compassionate empathy with our uniquely human lot. Look at this world, created for us to be human in! Even the act of looking at it gives it an appearance to our detriment or in our favour, depending on the state of our heart and the voluntary composition of our mind. Imagine the world, as a vibrant symphony or as an object of greed, as something to be discovered or as something to be criticized, as a tunnel of doom and indifference or as an ongoing adventure fit for a spirit of courage and enterprise – and that is how you shall have it. Apart from how you perceive it, the world is as nothing to you. You may once have been born into the light of day, which is the light of the world, but now that you listen to what I say to you, it may dawn on you how meanwhile you have darkened that light, rather than discovering the world in it, the world as it is and can appear to you when you understand it with your singular faculties and approach it for reasons no one else except you could invent."

55

If we come to an educator and he senses that our minds are negatively constructed or that we have bad habits of cowardly feeling and timid sentiment, he will naturally feel inclined to break those constructions down and to condemn us because of those habits. He can see how we are our own worst enemies and his tendency is always initially to destroy that enemy so that we may be liberated. But how can he condemn us and at the same time give us a taste for life? Will he not end up sacrificing our mind to our body, or our body to our mind?

We must come to terms with the fact that there is a cowardly thinking just as there is a cowardly feeling, and – that there is an arrogant feeling just as there is an arrogant thinking. What happens frequently these days is that bogus educators confront people who have run aground in terms of arrogant thinking, which thinking did at first seem most satisfying to them but now the unavoidable has happened so that the individual is stuck in a dead thought system of his own making or connivance – and the bogus educator breaks this system down, and then what comes to light, as if by magic, and often as a great wonder, is arrogant feeling, which seems to satisfy as much as the arrogant thinking initially did, but which will mislead its host into the same dead end. Where there was a lack of energy there is now abundant energy. But where there was no strength there is now still no strength. Similarly an alteration may be brought about from cowardly thinking, which at first satisfied as a semblance of kindliness but then betrayed, into cowardly feeling, which seems sublime but is no more than a 'high', an ecstasy or high spirits, which will eventually also betray.

So let's be very careful before we accept, or even buy, what someone is pleased to call an enlightenment experience. Arrogance and cowardice are bad, are worthless and detrimental, whether we nurture them thoughtful or emotionally. Remember, we may be taken in by both of these, not only because so much pleasure, albeit cheap or morbid pleasure, comes along with them at first before the rot sets in, but also on account of social bias in connection with them. A society may, on the whole, be fond of energy, even to the point of worshipping it, or it may be sceptical, downright suspicious of it. In reality energy is neither good nor bad and it makes as little sense to look for it as to avoid it. We are wise to learn how to cope equally well in the presence or the absence of it. But while we attach negative or positive value to energy we are likely to be taken in by cowardly or arrogant feeling or thought, and all the more by the one of these if once we have suffered shipwreck in one or run aground in the other.

And dressing up energy as aliveness and health, as love and self-expression, does not change it one whit, no more than defining the absence of it as deadness and illness, as tiredness, indifference and boredom.

The genuine educator does not tear us out of an inability and deposit us in a disability. Anything we do that is based on energy, for example, is disabling, even if we mistake it for health or love. It disables *us* as much as those who are taken in by our arrogance or cowardice.

In order to be guarded against bogus educators we might remind ourselves that our potential soul, not our psyche, is visible as our mind or invisible as our body, and then we will perhaps be less likely to mistake our flesh for our body or our spirit for our mind. And while we mistake our psyche for soul we are not even accessible to a soul and are pitched from one extreme of mood to the other.

What the genuine educator does when he comes up against our inabilities, such as all the forms of cowardice and arrogance, is manifest corresponding abilities. It is not enough to say that generally he practices courage and humility, because that makes him a mature adult but not yet an educator. In order to be an educator he must let my particular form of arrogance and cowardice affect him so that his response to me will be a courage and humility that is particular and peculiarly suited to me. He transforms my type of cowardice into his type of courage for my sake. He transforms my kind of arrogance into his kind of humility, for my sake. He is creative.

56

This transformation deserves to be looked at more closely.

The educator senses cowardice or arrogance and he ascertains which it is. Then he decides: is it mental or bodily, is it more to do with thinking or more with emotion and feeling. He condemns nothing, he only notices, observes and names. He senses instinctively. To him it seems as if the arrogance or cowardice were his own disability at that moment, and he may even react arrogantly or cowardly before he takes proper stock of the situation, but then he sees appearances for what they are and makes his adjustment. Every time he must say to himself: "Am I not here precisely for the purpose of exchanging this disability for an ability? Is it not my task as an educator to stand my ground as a mature human being and to conquer this arrogance and this cowardice for the sake of this one in front of me?"

In that way he re-establishes his authority which may for the moment have been shaken.

And is he not within himself on intimate terms with the one who would always draw us towards maturity? The one thing he knows that allows him to call himself an educator is that he himself stands constantly within the universal educational influence. If his authority has been momentarily shaken, all he needs to do is step back under that educational influence, in other words: to reaffirm his stature as an educator. It may seem to him that he exerts himself, or that he removes himself, depending on whether he has been affected by cowardice or arrogance, and he knows that it 'seems' one or the other. The soul whose disability of inability he has taken upon himself is neither entirely body nor entirely mind, and his ambition is that the two should become one, as communality and in communication. So he looks forward to something greater than this important removal of an inability, and that is the establishment of an actual ability in its place. The bogus educator merely substitutes a pleasant error for an unpleasant one, and he has his reward. His popularity and his money accumulate for the time being. The genuine, creative educator knows intuitively that as he allows the disability-affect to come to nothing in himself and as he overrides the inability-affect in himself, the one whose education he has at heart makes an actual leap forward in his soul, becoming more able. How this ability will eventually manifest itself, mentally and bodily (physically), or spiritually and carnally (concretely) – in other words what the one who is being educated will eventually be and do in terms of this ability, this does not concern the educator for the time being. He will have his reward and he knows it. His main ambition was that ability and more ability should be brought about, and we have seen how he has inwardly behaved so that it might come about. He has allowed himself to be affected by inability and disability and then he has, so to speak, furthered his own education, in the light of the one he himself uniquely knows, who can then establish ability in the one whose education the educator undertook.

57

We will say something about arrogance and about cowardice, as bodily or mental manifestations.

Mental arrogance, as a disability, before it has turned into an inability, is pleasurable in that it gives us a heightened sense of self and a false sense of well-being. It can come upon us suddenly and virtually sweep us off our feet, so that we experience lightness – only we do not really experience it but we have, as I say, a sense of it. An intensity, a vibrancy and buoyancy characterize that sense – only that it is not really character but mere attribute. We tend to attribute heightened awareness, but we are quite wrong to do that. We would do better to attribute emptiness and admit to ourselves that no matter how good this emptiness feels for the moment, and how tempted we feel to attribute to it all sorts of positive values – all the same, we would prefer fullness.

This is mental arrogance as a disability. It disables us, who harbour it, and those around us who are infected by it. We infect them by indulging ourselves in it, by acting it out and expressing it, as self-expression. Self-assertiveness is precisely such an indulgence. We mistake it for authority. Self-expression we mistake for creativity. Momentary opinions and ephemeral notions appear like truths and we preach them because to us they glow. Our heart is not touched, and yet this arrogance comes from the heart; (not from our heart, but from the heart; if it were *our* heart it would not give vent to these scintillating, sparkling, phosphorescent effusions.).

In our behaviour and in our language we manifest this mental arrogance and at first it feels good. It seems just and great. The educator makes no judgments concerning arrogance according to the behaviour or language of others. He observes this behaviour and language and pays heed in himself, watching for signs of arrogance such as we describe them here. Then he deals with that arrogance on behalf of those he would educate.

Not all arrogance is evident as a disability. But we must know it and recognize it in that initial state of cosy effusiveness, of ebullient attractiveness, of narcissistic self-advertisement. There is also an arrogance of the body, and we will come to that. Mental arrogance shows up in language and behaviour. The educator does not say: "Here is someone who talks arrogantly, I will tell him to stop being arrogant." He says: "Here is someone who is looking to be educated by me and in his company I am tempted to talk arrogantly, which means I can begin to educate by transforming that disability into an ability for that person." Even those of us who are not educators know fine well how foolish it is to condemn someone, and how tolerant we become once we have cleared up in ourselves the faults we saw in one another. A genuine educator makes consequential use of that insight.

Eventually mental arrogance as a disability burns out. It then becomes an inability. We cannot function any more, or only partially, in terms of language and behaviour. I, at this very moment, am suffering such an inability, and, looking back, I am able to recall how it began as disability, as I indulged in energetic self-expression while playing the piano, which gave me a great sense of self-evidence for several days. I was pleased with myself due to a heightened sense of meaning. I felt so much more spiritually alive but neglected to discern the nature of the spirit. I used music to inebriate myself and actually abused music and myself, not to mention the piano and those who listened to me and admired me. I infected them with my mental arrogance and their admiration of me and of the species of performance I perpetrated showed how I had infected them.

The inability set in while I rubbed my hands, not very energetically, and began as a slight pain between my shoulder blades. Within half a day it had intensified to the degree that only with severe pain could I move my arms at certain angles, and my neck became stiff. It was an agony to rise out of a chair. I have since submitted myself to that educator who has said: 'Your faith will heal you,' and have begun to improve. What I write down here by way of creative confession is also helpful. I have also decided to fast for a day, for clarification of the metabolic processes.

58

Usually when we use the word arrogance we describe someone who assumes power where he has no right. Mental arrogance therefore implies an illegitimate movement, by the back door, as it were, into a realm of thought that would not even exist except for a lack of patience, greed, vain ambition, and especially presumptuousness. One presumes upon territory to which one has no claim because the right path to it has not been chosen. An arrogant person is careless of others, and an arrogant realm of thought really excludes others, except insofar as they wish to be enslaved. Sometimes we like to be enslaved by someone's arrogant mind because, again, we get from it that pleasure peculiar to any disability. An educator must be thoroughly acquainted with this. He must be able to sense within himself, at a moment's notice, that digression to a mentality that is without basis, not in time or just plain ill-starred. He listens to how he expresses himself and observes his behaviour so that common sense and normality hold sway. He cannot tell if someone else is devoid of commonsense or abnormal because no standards exist for normality and common sense. He can, however, tell of himself, because he and no one else is the originator of his behaviour and language. Already he detects the tendency to arrogance in himself, when he wants to hold forth at the expense of communication, for example, or when he wants to ride roughshod over the opinions of others. If he is mature at the time, then he recognizes this tendency to arrogance in himself as transferred to him and he transforms it as such. If he cannot recognize it as transferred, he acknowledges to himself his own immaturity and lays himself open to the educational influence that is always available to him. Remember that someone who is immature must once have been mature, and knows therefore, of that influence, out of which he has strayed.

There is a bodily arrogance, which is an arrogance of emotion and feeling. If we are not so well acquainted with our body as with our mind we may well make the mistake all the more readily here of taking good feelings and much emotion for anything other than a pleasurable disability that is headed for breakdown. Good feelings are meaningless, and yet we make much of them if we are not careful. Much emotion is no guarantee of anything, and yet we suppose ourselves privileged at times if we are much moved, without questioning what moves us or wondering about the direction of the movement.

Now we cannot see the emotion or feeling of another. What is visible at times is what that person thinks or expresses of his feeling or emotion. Also we have a sense of his sentiment or imagination, where mind is combined with body. But of someone's emotion or feeling as such we cannot have any visible indication or test. But, of course, of our own emotion and feeling we are intimately conscious and perhaps even aware. Remember, we do not sense our emotion or feeling. It cannot be sensed. We are conscious or aware of it. What we do sense is behaviour and language, which is mind, and visible, or sensible. Our sensibility is no good for feeling and emotion, since it is itself bodily, and our body does not advance upon itself.

Arrogance of emotion and feeling is our presumption, by us ourselves, of our body as something we can sense. We know now that this is physically illegitimate; just as illegitimate as the presumption that we can think our own mind, hidden from view and not visible as behaviour and language. And yet these illegitimate experiences are frequently and by many sought out. Practices and so-called disciplines abound that are to help us attain to such illegitimate experiences, where mind is promised as immediate experience and body as sensed experience. In that way we hope to avoid the difficulty of joining mind and body as an operational soul that ends in works and functions creatively. This difficult way leads through a narrow opening and before we may enter we must have rid ourselves of much useless baggage, through moral and ethical action, and this takes time, effort, and infinite patience and care. True moral and ethical action and passion prepares us legitimately for what we would otherwise attempt to attain to illegitimately, by trickery and fast, when we are willing to sense our emotion and feeling or to be conscious or aware of our thought.

59

Before we can spot arrogance that is bodily, we have to have a fairly clear notion of legitimate consciousness and even awareness of emotion and feeling. Only then can we hold the illegitimate or arrogant body against that for the sake of correct identification. If we are to be educators, of whatever kind or species, we cannot afford to be on unsure ground here.

To be conscious of emotion means to know that it exists. If joy is an emotion, then here we can see that emotion has come into contact with thought in a certain way, so that in joy we have something greater than emotion. Calling joy an emotion is therefore technically not correct. We would do better to call it a form of life. The same goes for sorrow.

An educator must be able to operate on the level of emotion prior to its contact with thought, because on that level arrogance can set in. And so with feeling too. Sometimes we suppose that happiness is a feeling, though happiness, technically, is, like joy, another form of life, and of forms of life, such as happiness, joy, sadness, sorrow, we cannot be conscious or aware, though we do well to be conscious and even aware of feeling and emotion.

Only in consciousness and perhaps awareness of emotion and feeling can we, for example, and at a kind of beginning, even tell the difference between those two. Observe, for example, that you can feel whatever you choose to feel, just as you can think whatever you choose to think, but you cannot 'emote'. So the difference between passive and active comes to light here. Emotion is passive while feeling is active. I do, in terms of my body, when I feel, or I allow myself to be done to, in terms of my body, when there is emotion.

So emotion is something that accumulates, but only, observe! because I have decided, consciously, that is should, for the time being, accumulate. If I have not so decided, then emotion may well up and swamp me, this or that emotion, such as wrath or wretchedness, and although I may like that at the time, because it satisfies my selfish will, it is nonetheless a disability and I do well to recognize it as such.

I may opt, then, for emotion rather than feeling, and I may have perfectly good reason for doing so, as we shall see later, but it will be emotion that accumulates while I am consciously aware of it and not the sort of thing that bursts out of me uncontrollably such as a fit of anger or a flood of tears. Notice, I do not say anger and tears, but a burst and a flood of them.

We have to be careful now when we talk about emotion as though it could be controlled. It matters a great deal what we mean by passivity. Passivity is not indifference. When we know, for example, that the only way we can reach a certain goal and have the benefit of something is by enduring what stands between it and us, then we may well decide for a passivity of our body, in the knowledge that emotion overcomes hindrances of that specific kind. We might prefer to feel, which is bodily activity, but in certain cases feeling will not achieve the necessary end and all our attempts to make headway by feeling turn into an agony. It can turn into a horrible experience if the time for emotion has come but we do not know how to be even conscious of emotion, perhaps because we have always supposed that feeling must do, that our body must be active. Or perhaps we can only imagine passivity as idleness or a giving up, so that our body as passive is shameful for us to contemplate and we avoid, out of ignorance, the one thing that would see us through.

Not many come to this impasse, but when they do, let them remember that all things are possible and that their body as passive is grace. Only the great educators can set us an example here and prepare the ground for us, even as it was cleared the first time for them.[1]

The time for emotion, for our body as passive, has come when feeling, our body as active, is no longer a viable proposition. But until then we may feel as we choose – which is not the same as saying that we can have whatever feelings we like. We may choose to feel whatever is real, and just as in the case of emotion what matters is that we remain consciously aware: in the case of emotion of what goes on and in the case of feeling of what we do. Once not only awareness but even consciousness lapses and we fall asleep to reality, emotions and feelings set in, and then we readily fall prey to arrogance, and to cowardice for that matter, because then we only have a semblance of body.

---

[1] See Christian Bible, Mark 14:36

It only remains to be said, on this issue of real feeling and emotion, that if we do not make a habit of feeling that which is real, and if we do not get in the way of accumulating real emotion, we have no foundation for experience and will continue to break down.

So the educator sets himself the task of identifying the influences of his time that destroy awareness and subdue consciousness. He does his best to steer clear of those. So, for example, in our time the mass media not only supply all who desire it with a steady steam – a mass – of feelings and emotions while at the same time, as a medium, undermining, subliminally, our very willingness to remain aware and conscious. Those who are not capable of feeling and emotion but who know only of feelings and emotions cannot, of course, understand how this should be so, and they will even suggest the mass media as a venue for education, which is a great pity, because what they bring about is infatuation on a grand scale.

60

This should give us enough of a notion of what is meant by our body, by emotion and feeling, so that we can plot the course of arrogance (and later perhaps of cowardice) as soon as it sets in, primarily in ourselves as educators. We know that when we notice it in ourselves it must have been transferred. I am thinking of us now not only as mature adults, but as mature adults who educate. It may happen then that bodily arrogance may become an issue for us, as disability, when it will seem attractive to us, or as inability, when it seems repulsive. At both instances we are consciously aware of our state of being and may notice, for example, that a blush of excitement comes over us, because we feel we are being admired or emulated. This is a feeling with which we can deal right away simply by <u>dismissing</u> it. The arrogance would begin as soon as we believed that feeling, accepted it as substantial and enjoyed ourselves in the possession of it. That is to say, the arrogance in ourselves would begin then and it would be high time that we began to take stock. But even in order to be able to dismiss that initial flush of exuberance, we have to acknowledge to ourselves that we are dealing here with a disability that has been transferred to us, and that it is a disability. Similarly it might occur to us that our task is exceptionally easy, so easy that our work is nearly automatic. This would be an emotion with which we can simply <u>dispense</u> until we experience once again the normal weight of responsibility; like the feeling of exuberance, this emotion stemmed from an arrogance that originated in those we intend to educate. They themselves had no notion of it and certainly we have no intention of blaming them for it. We only want to make sure that we ourselves do not accidentally believe it, and the best way to make certain of that lies in our believing that we can simply dispense with it, and of this practical believing we can make a good habit. If our faculty of believing is fully occupied like this, we will not even be tempted by indulgence and infatuation. While we believe that all things are possible, no disability of the body can encroach upon us, no matter how pleasant it feels or how flattered we are by it.

61

Dismissing a feeling for the sake of feeling; dispensing with an emotion for the purpose of emotion: this is easy for some and not so easy for others. Disability feelings and emotions, compared to inability feelings and emotions, are attractive, so naturally we like them. We tend to give in to them and we incline to follow them up. The sheer magic of it excites us. We can get into a trance and even try to achieve them, to bring them on. An adult knows what this leads to, in general, namely break-down, but in the particular even an adult will time and again catch himself, during the course of some new exploration of some aspect of the world, trying to make up for a lack of real success or progress by indulging in some attractive disability. As soon as he notices what has happened he will condemn this in himself as immaturity and despise it. But that does not get rid of the poison in his system. It does not liberate him from the bad habit. Both the ordinary adult and the adult as educator are on the same ground here, though in the former the disability is acquired while in the latter it has been transferred to him. I mention this only so that we can keep in front of us the specific case of the educator's activity and experience. The dismissal and the dispensation we mentioned have to amount to more than a wish to be rid of something despicable. We will come to this same problem whether we have to do with disability or inability, with arrogance or cowardice.

The key to the solution of the problem lies in our conscious awareness. We can, at any given moment, choose to be consciously aware of our body, which is after all a body of knowledge. But we must in fact choose to do this, and do it, if our faculties are to be withdrawn from their erroneous investment.

But we do have help. A natural affinity exists between our conscious awareness and our true body of knowledge, and we are perfectly free at all times, no matter how enthralled we are otherwise by emotions and feelings, to take advantage of that affinity. If we want to be consciously aware of our body as feeling and emotion we do not have to search for a way to bring this about but we can simply let it happen. It may come as a marvellous surprise, akin to a release from bondage.

But of course who would believe, nowadays, that such an affinity exists, when the woods are full of privately guaranteed and publicly attested methods for making the wrong things happen, for shifting the ground which is no ground but sand? Who would believe it! – Well, those who believe it.

Are you able to be consciously aware? Do you have a body of knowledge? Then believe that the two are meant for each other.

62

What we have now is a tool in the educator's hand, for him to use as soon as he experiences transferred arrogance or cowardice of the body. So far we have only touched on the arrogance, and only on arrogance as a disability, which is attractive, seductive and flattering. As soon as such feelings or emotions rise in the educator, he takes note and then simply switches over to conscious awareness of his own feeling and emotion, that is to say, to his body, which is his body of knowledge, live and invisible. In that way he successfully dismisses and dispenses with that false body, which is really an impostor.

And, of course, the example he sets of someone who can do that and in fact does it, in the company of those who are much more accustomed to having their emotions and feelings empowered by someone who rejects or welcomes them, is all important, because live emotion and feeling is transported, by the educator, for and to those whom he wishes to educate.

In the company of the educator, then, what we experience is freedom. We do not so much experience a liberation from emotional hang-ups or from complications of feeling, which would not be experience at all but an irrelevant side-issue, but we have actual experience of freedom itself, which is substantial and concrete. Freedom is experienced in terms of itself, not of pleasure or pain.

The bogus educator would switch us from mental inability to a liberated body, or from inabilities of feeling and emotion to a liberated mind. First of all he does not recognize disability as something to be obviated, so he concentrates only on inability. Then by switching from body to mind or from mind to body he merely transposes, so that a disability, which he mistakes for freedom, takes the place of an inability. Of freedom he knows nothing.

63

The inabilities of our body are not pleasant but unpleasant. When emotion does not flow we become temperamental, recalcitrant and truculent. When feeling is not expressed we become joyless, unaffectionate and indifferent. Our senses cease to function properly, vision disappears, imagination turns into accidental pictures.

Every inability was once a disability. This is like saying that every 'low' was once a 'high'. Where unpleasant emotions torture us, such as a streak of cruelty, there we may assume did once exist a pleasant emotion, such as a sweet seductiveness. But knowing this doesn't help us because both disabilities and inabilities have to be tackled on their own ground, or rather on their own lack of ground. It takes us a long enough time to discern between emotions and emotion, between feelings and feeling, between sensuality and sensuousness, in other words between the broken body and our new body. We notice the crippling emotions in ourselves, the harshness, the sudden rages, the perplexing break-downs in our relation to one another and the world, and it frightens us. We scare ourselves. We are appalled by what we suspect we might do. Our feelings of nausea, of impotence and worthlessness, threaten us and we tend to make matters worse by defending ourselves against them. We try to control the emotions, to resist the feelings and to lie to ourselves about them. As soon as we understand them as inabilities we may take kindly to the good news that for each one of them a corresponding ability exists, somewhere in ourselves, though on a slightly different plane, so that we can not, so to speak, look straight across from the inability to the ability, but first we must let go of that particular inability, even as we sense it, and of course we cannot manage that, as we mentioned earlier in reference to bad habits, unless we first trust that we can be returned, and will be returned, automatically, to our healthy bodily functions, or rather to our healthily functioning body, and an influence does always and everywhere exist for our benefit, which is good love. This influence of good love on all of us operates at all times and all that remains for us is to know that it exists. But that does remain for us. Unless we take account of it, it works alright, but not in our personal favour.

64

Inabilities of emotion, feeling and sense can therefore be left behind by us once we have identified them as inabilities, as soon as we acknowledge to ourselves that we are always being influenced by a spirit of good love.

An educator acts within a certain cultural, social and communal environment. He therefore takes upon himself the body inabilities of that environment. An evil emotion may frequently seek him out, or a feeling of condemnation. He may sense so critically that the world becomes a desert for him and all mankind an abomination. The better educator notices these inabilities earlier in himself, and like any adult he asks himself: What can I do about them? If he knows himself as to some extent an educator, though he may be most active as a choreographer, as a maker of artworks or as a philosopher, he will recognize these inabilities as transferred and then he will transform them in his own works. The teacher in front of a class of youngsters is overcome by a sense of defeat and, upon taking stock, he feeds that experience creatively into the curriculum. Just as a painter who is persuaded of personal worthlessness does not say: "First I must rid myself of this inability and then maybe I can begin my next artwork," so does the teacher in front of a class not say: "First I must suppress this sense of being defeated and then I can go on with my instruction." Both realize that their work has already begun when they identify that transferred inability. Creativity is willing to bear that burden for the sake of others as a good work. Creativity thrives on our conscious awareness of a perpetual influence of good love.

65

We mentioned the affinity of our conscious awareness and of our body of knowledge. Now we spoke of our conscious awareness of a perpetual influence of love. So we notice here how our conscious awareness is like the mediator between that love and our body. However – and this is a major consideration – personality, and therefore another one or two, must be involved. To put it as simply as possible, unless we love one another, that perpetual influence of love on us cannot be accepted by us.

And so the educator too, who experiences in himself transferred arrogance and cowardice, makes it his central and intentional principle to love those he wishes to educate, and then his conscious awareness will work, in affinity with his body and in acceptance of that influence, that creative influence, of good love.

66

We have dealt with our human body chiefly in terms of emotion and feeling. Just recently we brought in the element of sense, which allows us to speak of our body as a body of knowledge. But of course emotion and feeling are equally knowledgeable. It might do to speak of inward knowledge, emotion and feeling, and of outward knowledge, sense. I steer away from speaking of sensation for a reason that should become clear.

Now since <u>sense</u> is a function of our new and whole body, arrogance and cowardice can occur in this department too, again either as immaturity in an adult, or as transferred in an educator or teacher. For now we will take a quick look only at arrogant sense and leave cowardly sense for later, when we deal with cowardly emotion and feeling.

In order to understand what is meant by arrogant sense, we have to come to terms with something that has become unfashionable with the advent of epistemology as a separate study. More to the point, what has become unfashionable is a certain predisposition of human beings which has in any case never been properly worked out. Simply stated, <u>sense is not sound unless substantiated by emotion and feeling.</u>

This means not that we are to sense something merely visual and ask ourselves how we feel about what we saw and then somehow bring sight and feeling into agreement so that the latter underpins the former. What it means is that nothing can properly make sense to us unless at the same time our emotion and feeling is involved, so that knowledge really gained implies an organically whole process of emotion-feeling-sense, where the inward knowing, emotion and feeling, is in fact what the outward knowing, the sense, rests upon. More specifically we can gain clarity by observing how emotion substantiates sense, feeling particularly supports sense, and sense rests on them both.

Which brings us into the vicinity of that which is sensed, in relation to which we can finally speak of sensation.

And our most suitable expression for what we soundly sense is, of course, reality. If, instead of reality, we say world, environment, others, things out there, we always make a partial reference, perhaps appropriate, to reality. But reality is that which is properly and soundly sensed, substantiated by feeling and emotion; and equally that which allows us to appreciate reality is sense as resting upon emotion and feeling.

67

Our sensation of reality is probably the most important experience of our lives. Once we have sensed reality, only the first and one time, we can never forget it. An experience of reality is etched into our memory. A description of such an experience might emphasize how inward and outward awareness become one and are not any more differentiable, while at the same time something new is sensed. We can say that reality is always sensed as new.

Another aspect of real sensation is its completeness, which is evident to us at that time. Note that it makes no difference in such a case whether we speak of real sensation, of a real sensation, or of a sensation of reality. In a sensation of reality, what strikes us is the completeness. We realize that this is finished. Painters are never done trying to reproduce this experience on canvas, because only by passing it on to others can we really make it our own. Real sensation is in fact something that goes on and that we do while we create a new work. I intentionally make no difference between artists and non-artist here. The context of the sensation of reality is another one, namely the one of the personal human being, who does what he does creatively, and should he do no more than weep.

We have gone some distance, on the preceding pages, towards an identification of disability and inability in the cases of the mind and the body, against a backdrop of our able mind and body. We spoke of disability and inability due both to arrogance and to cowardice. Just as we were about to concern ourselves with cowardly feeling and emotion, that other bodily function presented itself, namely sensation. So here too we must identify disability and inability, cowardice and arrogance. We can do so, now that we have given some indication of what is meant by sound, or real, sensation.

Arrogant vision (or sensation) takes into account all that lies outside our senses, so that we actually project something like a myth of reality beyond the pale of what we then might call the everyday experience or the trivial foreground. In reality nothing lies outside our senses; there is no outside or inside to our senses. But arrogance tempts us to presume such

103

an outside, beyond a border set up for that purpose. Our body, as a consequence, has to undergo a violation because while sense strains out there, emotion and feeling are 'left behind' or 'escaped from'. It feels great to be rid of the sick man in the house. Little do we realize that the sick man is ourselves. So we entertain, with increasing vigour, a vision of 'reality out there', of 'this world', because our seeming reward is liberation from emotion and feeling which was actually not at all problematic until we strove to leave it behind. The arrogance comes first, as a simple temptation to sense 'out there', and to make something of the exciting prospect that seems to offer itself to our perceiving self. Then emotion and feeling 'complain' so to speak, like a wife who insists she is being ignored by her husband. The arrogant husband insists he shall go out; secretly he wants to get away from the complaining wife, little realizing that she complains because he has begun to stray.

68

We can take it for granted that prior to the temptation of what we might call 'the reality beyond', (which should really be called the falsehood), sensation, emotion and feeling are one. We could not say that emotion and feeling substantiate sensation, or that sense rests on emotion and feeling, because that is not the case until the great falsehood is found out for what it amounts to and for what it does not amount to. But the alienation of sense from emotion and feeling, so that we can speak, in retrospect of course, of outside experience and of inside experience (none of which is really experience) is a definite temptation into which we stray – and the educator or teacher is aware of this. It is most crucial that he knows of it, because a., he must not try to prevent it by any outside measures, meeting the falsehood on its own terms and b., he will continue to present the truth of the matter, by again and always introducing sense and sensation to feeling and emotion, bringing the two into relation, joining the affective and the effective nature of what he presents as worthy of attention.

What counts for the educator is that there is a separation of sense from emotion and feeling in those he wishes to educate, and that consequently he himself will find transferred to himself a load of arrogant sensation, but also of corrupt emotion and spoiled feeling. He can understand the reason for this in terms of the almost unavoidable temptation to sense arrogantly, to try to grasp a false reality that presents itself as somehow 'out there', or simply 'there', as outside the senses and therefore to be conquered by the senses, or by someone by means of sensation alone, separate from feeling and emotion.

That which is thought of, or imagined, as 'reality out there' by the tempted individual promises not only a release from deserted emotion and feeling, which are now experienced as inside, but it also promises a final solution to all mortal concerns, to the problems of time and to the limitations of space. The wicked encouragement is always to "try just that little bit harder and everything will fall into place".

Our western civilization is most beset by an arrogance of sense experience, while the eastern affliction is more one of cowardice, which we intend to speak of later.

Our scientific and technological advances can in fact only be called advances in the direction away from reality and towards an ultimate conquest of a falsehood out there, which is said to be objectively real but in reality does not even exist. The efforts that lead to true cultural advances spring from a new establishment of sense experience on feeling and emotion, which come alive and are in fact live as soon as they are enrolled again to substantiate and support good sense.

Arrogant sensation as a disability fills us with notions of a cumulative success out there and of a permanent escape from crippling subjectivism and the whining psyche. There is something like an inebriation with empire, with empirical doctrine, with objectified harmony of the world, with the ambition to get the elements permanently under control, enslaved, eating out of our hand. Human beings are viewed as transcendental visionaries inter-attached via telecommunication. An angelic dimension lures us on and we hope to shed our humanity, because by now we definitely experience it as a curse – like the madman, who wants to fly off a cliff, experiences the rope that ties him to a tree as a curse. This arrogance disability is readily confused with heady inspiration, with genus, and the masses of people long for its prodigious achievements. But in each individual instance it has to burn out. 'The world in flames' is the general catastrophe, while the collapse of individuality attends each individual case.

The educator also holds out a promise, and his promise is greater than the one we associate with standard ideals and prizes. What he promises draws us down and away from the addiction to research into everything out there – because above all he loves us. For the educator, love is the principle instrument of restitution. Not love as a sensation, as an emotion or as a feeling, of course. Most of us would not right away know what was left. What else can love be, once you have taken out the sensation, the emotion and the feeling?

The creative educator knows love quite simply as the creative and recreative strength par excellence. And crucially important, he accepts that he cannot fully understand it or entirely embrace it with any of his faculties. It surpasses his understanding and all his faculties. He knows that this love exists in reality and that he himself can partake of it, participate in it, do it and act it out. Happily he acknowledges that because of this love he is truly able to educate.

69

What the educator promises is that we can let go of our outside sensations and still carry on, though for a while we may well be confused. But in that confusion we know, thanks to the educator's efforts, or even due to his presence alone, that we are safe. This sense of security is important, because without it we would continue to insist on external (or internal, as we learn in the case of cowardice) experience as real. We cannot find our way back to our emotion and feeling without such a sense of security. Our emotions would play up terribly, and our feelings would shock us, because, let's face it, our entire complex of orientation is to be rearranged. Our senses have been trained to external data and our emotions and feelings (consequently, though we would hardly admit this) had turned into something we would rather not know about. Our pride is built on how we get on among a welter of falsehoods which we take for real goods. Our sense of self is built on the way we relate to that which in truth is irrelevant. Even as children in school we were bombarded with outside data and trained like performing seals in the manipulation of them. How much we need to forget! The creative educator can help us forget. We need to trust him. He may say many things that seem absurd to us but they are intended as comforts, to help us while we turn away from the outside darkness and towards the reality within and among us.

This reality within and among us becomes evident to us as we learn to respond to the specific love expressed by the creative educator. Since it is a love that demands nothing, and certainly not requital, we are left free to choose. Personality begins to play into the very first possibilities of communal sensation.

This communal sensation creeps upon us when we cannot tell. When we least look for it – we have done it. But suddenly it will seem important to us that the person next to us is given the advantage we ourselves would like. We think of the person next to us as though he were ourselves. We love him as ourselves. I begin to treat you as though you were I. You have trouble with a locked door? I offer to help as though I

107

myself had that difficulty. This is quite different from my helping you because I suppose I should or because I am a busybody who does not understand that every problem suits the one who has it and who misunderstands all difficulties as mere entanglements in outside sensations as annoying checks to arrogance which must be removed so that arrogance may once again blossom.

The teacher in the classroom helps the pupil back out of his arrogance-entanglements by involving him secretly in communal sense. He brings his personality to bear on the pupil even though that pupil may not be capable of any personality. To the pupil it seems almost as if he were being isolated, encapsulated in himself, incapable for a while of expression or comprehension, but all the same 'at home in himself', in a way not any more familiar to him or not yet familiar to him. We might say that the immature adult is educated back to his maturity while the child or youth is educated ahead towards his maturity.

70

When the disability of arrogance has 'flourished' for a while it must take its toll, because the body is literally torn in two, as sensation parts from emotion and feeling, and then in three, as emotion and feeling also separate. The energy just simply runs out. We see children, very young, who bounce back and forth between disability, overactive and extrovert, and inability, dull, sullen and introvert, with a rapidity that testifies to their natural resilience. The educator learns to distinguish between arrogance and cowardice, between inability and disability. He observes, allows the affect to transfer and deals with it as though it were his own but knowing it as transferred.

Where arrogant sensation as disability is accompanied by a pleasant delusion of 'being in control', as inability it is accompanied by an unpleasant delusion of losing control. We

108

strive to regain control but things get worse. The nerves give out, the hormones go wrong, blood pressure is high or low, we feel useless, worthless and downcast. The educator in our presence (if we are so lucky as to have one in our presence) manages a steady profile. Both the unpleasant and the pleasant delusion he encounters in himself and he recognizes them for what they are worth, as delusions. He has something to offer that overrides them. And he offers it. Let's call it love expressed and comprehended as a sense of communal reality.

Arrogant sensation as an inability is a misery. The individual is forced to countenance the vanity of his ways. In vision, that is to say in all of his senses, he strives to regain his precarious hold on the disability experience of former times, he cannot help but compare the empty vanity now to the full vanity then. Of course he is closer to the truth than he was, because at least his experience of vanity is correct. He does not mistake a sow's ear for a silk purse. But what consolation can he draw from being closer to the truth? Misery wells up in him, as resentment and bitterness. He is no more to blame for what he goes through now than for what he went through then. What can he see except appearances drained of all life? His eye that previously sparkled so charismatically, is empty of light. His ear hears only the shell of speech. What he touches persuades him of the insubstantiality of all reality and he curses it.

This is the time when it enters his head that he might, if he chose, assure himself of a modicum of reason by perpetrating a purely technological advance. The educator does well to step in at this point. His heart goes out to the one who is unable to function soundly and sanely and he would dearly like to be able to explain to him how within the context of his misery, of bitterness and resentment, he is only one hair's breadth away from religion, which is to say: from the communal life, from which he once distanced himself through the arrogance of supposing that sensation out there, away from emotion and feeling, could possibly amount to anything other than loss of humanity.

And yet, as the educator contemplates the miserable individual, understanding full well how tempting and what a lure the empty 'out there' can be, he is equally conscious of the joyful experience in store for that individual, which is greater than anything he might have known had he never been tempted. The one who has strayed and returns is richer for the experience.

From the vantage point of this special joy the educator makes his successful appeal. How important, that this intimate understanding of the advantage at stake is kept alive by the educator in himself! He feels in himself the downcast spirit of the unfortunate individual, who has perhaps made a way of life out of his inability, resigned to it and justifying it, and at the same time he knows what joy is in store for the one who confesses his inability, who says: "Yes, I am miserable, because within myself I am dead, and this is unfortunate, so I wish it were otherwise. Surely I have it within myself to learn how to cancel the hindrances in my nature to the free flow of life, of joy and happiness, which I see exemplified in my teacher. After all I am an adult human being and my human nature should carry me through thick and thin. So what, if I have, over a period of time, forfeited my humanity by giving into the temptation to sense 'that which is not real'. Now has come the time to reverse the order of my existence, to look within myself, patiently and soberly, for that wellspring of humanity so long neglected and nearly dried up."

The educator knows how to encourage him: "I can show you by my own example that humanity is an excellent experience in itself. Once you have the hang of it, reality will never again escape you. But humanity comes first. Get around to imagining it as something other than an abstraction, in case you have acquired that bad habit. Imagine yourself to be a river that flows in a bed of humanity. Imagine yourself as a tree that grows in the soil of humanity. Or imagine that the air you breathe is humanity itself. In this way you will make some good use of this gift called imagination. Perhaps you have lost faith in humanity, which is quite understandable. Experience it now, and first of all with your senses. Don't tell me that you can't see humanity because it isn't out there. That's why you missed it, because it isn't out there. Humanity is the essence of being; you have not yet been. Or perhaps once you were, but then you lost conscious awareness of it. Believe that you can see what you wish to see. How else can the light come back into your eye, the sound into your ear, the touch into our fingertips? Within your human nature all the secret ingredients lie ready. Your senses have become divorced from our human nature. You turned them into mechanical data processors, and you were just about to add another dimension to that infernal machine in terms of technical expertise. What were you going to do? Did you suppose you might function out there on borrowed space and time? For how long?"

The pupil in the classroom is not an adult but his senses are disturbed by the same temptation, since he lives among immature adults and readily tends in any direction that promises an outlet for raw energy and an indulgence in crude sensation. The pupil in the classroom is a child whose senses are nevertheless much more open to change than those of that adult who frequently makes up his mind to a third-rate existence and takes pride in abiding by those convictions. There is no equivalent among children to the stiff-necked adult. So the teacher in the classroom recognizes the sensual arrogance inability and – overlooks it. He literally ignores it a he concentrates on his own humanity, so that the miserable child, the bitter and resentful child, will not at all find his inability resisted, challenged or criticized, while the teacher appeals to his humanity by concentrating on his own. Whatever the teacher relates to the pupil is first sensed by the teacher in relation to his own humanity, and not in relation to anything out there. And nothing should be related to the pupil, by the teacher, unless the teacher has first of all made that human connection with it, where he can honestly say to himself that it does make sense to him. It must make sense to him in person, and not on hearsay or merely because he has to present it as an item of the curriculum.

The teacher has a thoroughgoing notion of his humanity.

does not confuse it with life. An important discrepancy comes to light here. The artistic function feeds on 'life'; the creative impulse draws on humanity. The difference between the artistic and the creative is therefore crucial when we come to discuss the role of the educator and teacher. What the artist calls life is not something to gain and have, but something to transcend. The artist immerses himself periodically in what he calls life, not because this life is something in itself for him but because it stimulates his procreative instinct so that he can then function artistically. Such artistic functioning is unique, and we can learn about the creativity so essential to education if we compare to it the artistry that has become such a modern counterfoil and 'mere' corrective to the arrogance and cowardice of our modern existence.

The secret of the comparison lies in what is meant by life. The artist means one thing, the creator means another.

71

Since this is a doctrine of creative, not of artistic, education, the life of the creative person, in other words: that which a creative person calls life, is more important to us, and from that point of view we look at what the artist calls life. Creativity is significant in terms of life because it predisposes the creative one for an increase of life, even as he himself draws on his humanity so that others should have life. He draws on something in himself, whereas the artist draws on, or rather feeds on, a kind of life, more like an aliveness, that he sees going on all around him and that resides in appearances. Once these appearances are copied, imitated or reproduced, the artist has done what he intends to do, though he knows that much else goes on besides, which he ascribes to his talent. The nature of this talent must always remain an enigma to him. He knows that he can trade it in for money without necessarily diminishing it, but then he has to admit that his own true wellbeing does not stem from the same source as his art, and so he is always to some extent torn. Teachers can approach their pupils artistically just as painters can approach their painting. Such teachers have a gift or talent for teaching, and they too are always torn between the quality of their product on one side and the quality of their 'life' on the other. Certainly there is always a kind of excitement, due to a transfer of energy, involved in every exercise of a gift, but this excitement takes its toll. Every satisfaction that is drawn from it shows up at some other time as a depletion, and only rarely are the two associated in the mind of the artist. He knows of the 'ups' and the 'highs' in his work as somehow reflective of the 'lows' and the 'downs' in his 'life', and vice versa, but he knows of no law that allows him to take a standpoint in equal relation to both. This reminds us, of course, of the disability and the inability we discussed earlier. The artistic gift or talent lends its possessor an immunity from both, but only while he reproduces and represents them as they appear all around him. The artistic activity lends the artist a temporary stability. He does not accumulate life. At best he accumulates art products. That which the creative teacher calls life, and which he himself accumulates at the moment, creatively, is the same as that which lures the artist. It might, for example, be "the eternally feminine or female that draws him anon", he might envision it, always in the future, in any number of guises. A female artist would readily look forward to it as 'the eternally masculine or male'.

What is of especial interest to us in this present book is how it might be possible for someone to switch from the artistic approach to life to a creative enjoyment of it. What is it that has to be renounced as that life may be gained? An artist takes pleasure from production, but at the same time he is, as we mentioned, torn between the pursuit of a future blessing and the experience of present desires. Production, as we said, temporarily bridges that gap without being instrumental in an accumulation of life. If it should occur now to someone who espouses an artistic existence, which is an existence based on pleasurable production of works of art in the widest sense of that word – including what a teacher might do in a classroom – if it should occur to him that he is fed up being strung out in terms of hope and desire, and if it dawns on him that there might be something better on the cards for him than this eternal self-sacrifice alternating with self-indulgence, so that again and again something is built up that has to be torn down again, then he might concentrate on his own humanity.

Until now he has been in conflict with his human nature. Now he has to understand that this human nature of his needs nothing added on to it that he can add on, and that it needs nothing taken away from it that he can take away. This understanding is crucial to him for the change he would undergo and it is a change he cannot bring about, but he must undergo it. The pleasure he derives from production has confirmed him in the habit of adding on to, and taking away from, his human nature in order to approximate it to an ideal, that lies ahead of him, or in order to retain it within the manageable bounds of an everyday existence. His adding on to his human nature is idealistic while his taking away from it is moralistic, And because he has come to associate an habitual pleasure with the working out of this moral ideal he is not very likely to give serious consideration to the creative suggestion that his human nature cannot really and in any permanent way gain from his productive manipulation unless – I say he is not very likely to give this thought serious consideration unless – he decides that the pain that comes along with the self-sacrifice outweighs the pleasure he associates with artistic production.

We cannot help thinking of the artistic or talented human nature as one that rushes ahead of its true happiness and is reluctant to let itself be shaped. Our human nature is itself productive of something, if we allow that to come about and if we wait patiently for it to happen, denying in ourselves that urge to make it happen, before the time is right. If we make it happen, the time is always wrong. In fact, the urgency we experience to make this happen – to make human nature reveal itself – can lead us directly to the point where we can recognize our human nature's true productivity – if we stem that urgency and set ourselves against it. What happens then, as soon as the time is ripe, is that our human nature produces humanity, on which we can then creatively draw.

72

A creative teacher in a classroom draws on his humanity and does not manipulate his human nature or the human nature of his pupil. As soon as he feels urged to ad to, or subtract from, human nature he stems that urgency. This is something that actually has to be done. To the creative teacher it would be a failure, to go ahead with artistic education, even though such education can look so much more attractive and feel so much better – dysfunctionally, that is to say, as a disability, or, more precisely, as a check to it and a reflection of it.

An artistic teacher who would wish to teach creatively would first of all wean himself off the pleasure he takes habitually in controlling his pupils (taking from their human nature) or in exciting them (adding to their human nature). But he would only succeed in this if he believed that eventually something greater than this pleasure was in store for him. We cannot rid ourselves of trivial passions unless we court great passion. Or, it would be enough to say: we cannot rid ourselves of passions unless we court passion.

And when we speak of the humanity that naturally comes about and is so to speak produced spontaneously by our human nature if we stem the urge and halt the drive of our nature to be diminished or augmented by us, the we mean passionate humanity. Once we draw on it, we have it as action, but prior to that we have it passionately.

So anyone who is fed up with being artistic and would like to become creative can in fact succeed if he aims for passionate humanity and does not stray from the conviction that what he tries to satisfy with artistic passions now, which will not hold, will be more than satisfied by passionate humanity if he holds out long enough – as long as it takes – in arresting his human natural urges and drives. These urges and drives are neither good nor bad, so it is pointless to praise or condemn them. But as soon as we begin to stem and halt them, to arrest them, we prepare in ourselves the ground for passionate humanity.

"However," says the artist, "what can I do while no such passions, such drives or urges, are upon me? You say that by arresting them I make room for humanity. What if none appear? What if, precisely because I am ready to arrest them, they remain in hiding? Should I not go ahead then and opt for excitement and control, for self-enhancement and self-control in myself and in the world and in those around me? If I stimulate here and subdue there, if I stir up and set up, interest and mollify, have I not a much better chance then to come up with something to arrest?"

What terrible nonsense! All the same, the question is important. While no passions, no derives or urges appear, the thing to do is not artificially to produce them but to espouse humanity with a will and if humanity is not yet an experience but only a word for you, or something you confuse with being humane, humanitarian or humanistic, then simply look forward to it as that which will make itself plain to you as soon as you have sufficiently longed for it and desired it. remember you must ask if you are to receive, you must receive if you are to have, and you must have if you are to hold. And humanity is the treasure of your life.

73

On the hinge of humanity turns the difference between these three: your standard man, your artist and your creator. Look at them all three side by side and come to the conclusion that here we have a line of ascent, and that while each of us must pitch his tent where he can, there all the same lurks a suspicion in our innermost recesses that without the creator the rest come unstuck. Your standard man has his rules and regulations, his recipes and catechisms. He knows top from below, left from right, swears there are none so complete as himself is and then disappears, simply, from the face of the earth. He would have his world solid, forever unchanging, resting on principle as on the back of an elephant, while a difference of opinion is sedition. Or he laughs if you argue, and says you deserve your damnation. When it comes to education he knows the one purpose: standards! Even the heavens are built on them four square. So let young people heed. An adult knows, has no need to learn. If you haven't the secret of success in your grasp by the age of twenty-five you stand exposed as a scoundrel, and as every standard man knows, the world is full of scoundrels. They are a menace to the status quo and must be shunned. Your standard man has raised the standard opinion, upon a pedestal – to show that you must be wrong if you differ. The reason for education, for a good and sound education, is plainly to separate the good men from the scoundrels, the decent from the suspect. Education, therefore, is largely a preaching of the unquestionable ancestral virtues and a practicing of the tried and tested traditional skill. Our standard man is an old man. Let those who grow up have the full benefit of learning how to be old. He does not 'grow' old, for growth is suspect; it smacks of change. The only safe growth adds inches.

Who comes along and redresses the balance? The artist. For the artist is young. He never grows up and he insists on it. Here comes the man of experiment, of exploration and exploitation. When he sits in government you may hold on to your seat because the ground is liable to tremble. He loves change, the artist does, and sometimes for its own sake. With a vengeance he clings to the ephemeral surfaces because look, he thrills to them. Is further justification needed? His task is to show to the standard man how fallible are standards. To that end the artist will engineer revolutions and improvise follies, and when you compare this only to what came before and to what is cast in relief by them you cannot defend ourself entirely against an onset of admiration. Only when you look at what follows do your clouds of doubt gather. You wonder, then, how could your artist survive, as artist, if it were not for your standard man? He must have him to react against. The artistic product, whether it is a political state, a brand of religion or a certain kind of painting or musical composition – or a method of educating – is neither trivial nor ponderous in essence, but reactionary. It must stand in opposition or not stand. When we talk about it, to plumb the meaning of it, we need to reflect on its circumstances and we do well to draw these into account.

Which is not to say that art products have a merely temporal effect. In their inception they are contrary, but they stand

and last, while they stand and last, as achievements. The virtue of them as achievements affects us as ambivalence and ambiguity. Your dyed in the wool standard man will shut his solid oak front door to that scoundrel artist and then invest in his product. Your typical artist will praise the standard man to his face and then undermine all his standards. In truth the artist is no more a scoundrel than the standard man is a pillar of substance; or from the other aspect, the standard man is no more a hollow gourd than the artist is a flame of truth. We must see the two of them in a kind of existential counterbalance if we are to – acquaint ourselves with creative men and women. Our book is about creative education, not about standard or artistic education, and creative education becomes possible because some men and women are willing and able to raise themselves above the back and forth of repeated history. They see the standard approach and it lacks an attention to growth, development and evolution. Then they look at the artistic approach and see that it lacks an appreciation of moral integrity and the sense of a sound goal. They themselves carry within themselves the germ of the new and effective. The standard man is not attracted by it and the artist only recognizes it once he feels he wants more than his artistry can gain him.

Eventually we will have to take a separate look at both standard and artistic education, if only to become more aware of what creative education is not. At the moment we would just remark that the creative person, who draws on his humanity rather than reacting to the standard life of appearances, is capable of an art too, but he makes use of it to aid his creativity. He would never be an artist and he achieves no art product, but what he does come up with is a creative representation of himself which serves him as a vehicle for the offering of his humanity to others. Creative men and women, for example speak a language that is an art work so that their communication should be a giving of life. A creative teacher would come up with art works to make his educational approach more palatable and interesting. We distinguish here between creative art works, originating in someone's individual humanity, and artistic works, or works of art, that testify to a social constraint and do not transfer life but exist to be admired and to entertain.

74

Our <u>cowardice</u>, like our arrogance, is not laid upon us but we entertain it every day. We sit in judgment upon one another on account of it, and because we would rather not know of it. And yet, if I would be an educator or a teacher in a classroom it won't do for me to pretend that cowardice is for me no affliction.

Beginning with my senses, and in reverse order now, leaving feeling and emotion to the last, I can say in full honesty that a vision of the truth makes me quake. What is more, I have spoken to others who confess to that same affliction. Either the truth has forever passed them by or they tremble when they know it. For the truth is so mighty in our hearts, by dint of the way we fit into this essence, that we cannot but take exception to the way it imposes upon us inordinately, and in areas of ourselves where we are not aware. Oh we suppose we should wish to be aware, but a barrier intervenes, something very much like a concrete impossibility, and though a feather would smudge it, we convince ourselves we have not the strength.

This almighty power of self-conviction, when it comes to a sense, to a vision of the truth, so that we 'know' we cannot do it, is a generation of cowardice. Not only do we know we cannot do it, but we are willing and eager to expend vast energies to prove that it cannot be done.

And all the time with the lightest of touches it could be managed, and our lives in the blink of an eye would be transformed.

Why is it that cowardice plays a role to the extent that our eyes will not open and our ears will not hear? What worries us about the truth? We would rather sweat daily in slavery to a world we ourselves have constructed in bold misconception than take one close look at the world that all readily exists. The world we wilfully imagine is never the real world, though we wear ourselves out attesting to the contrary. We cannot bear it that something exists that is perfect when we ourselves are evidently so imperfect. But no, not evidently. Not to ourselves in any case. If once we admit we are half we begin to grow whole. No, the heart and soul of our cowardice is that we insist we are whole, and more than whole, when in truth we are quarters and eighths. Indeed the smallest fragment may make the largest claim to a sovereign completion, though from a truthful point of view every utterance is plain vanity.

Understandable that we fear the truth because it highlights our falseness. With every fresh approach of the truth, with every welling up of it inside us as living water, we flinch and shrink. There is no cowardice in that; it is simple arithmetic. An increase of light to the eye makes that organ contract and the lid comes down. If the world that is were suddenly forcefully revealed to us, quite irrespective of our readiness for that experience, the shock would wipe us out. Happily there are some safeguards at the start, so that the change comes on slowly. Repeatedly there are flashes of light, enough to make it dawn on us that something is desirous of our attention being drawn to it, but honestly, we would much rather sleep. And in our sleep we concoct all those reasons, clever and subtle ones if plain down to earth ones won't do, as to why there is no such thing as the truth, or if there is, why we cannot be held responsible for allocating the resource of it or making it our loadstar.

And therein lies the cowardice. It stretches and yawns, and then returns us to the task of proving that falsehood is greater than truth, that it can in fact quite blot it out. And why should it not, since the truth is effectively a menace? Look how we feel in the presence of the thing! Our faces are twisted sarcastically while our hands reach for stones. We act like wild men, behave like fools, become hysterical, throw fits and tantrums – all that for a start. We would rather kill the truth than admit it exists. And many a man is right when he says: "There is no truth," because he has killed it. Happily no one can kill it for another but for ourselves we can do the job outright. And then of course we will not take kindly to those who have still a fresh appetite for the truth.

75

When we look more closely at how we use our senses, we discover how often we actually sense for no other reason than so that the way we are presently will be factually justified. If we are presently wicked, for example, then we look for examples of wickedness all around us – and we find them. Not that we know or admit we are wicked, though we are. But the sum-total of our sensing is concerned with detecting only that which is most like ourselves, so that in this case we see wickedness everywhere, though of course we give it an acceptable name. Just as arrogant sensation posits experience 'out there' and makes a point of recognizing it exclusively, so does cowardly sensation recognize only experience we like, experience of things and states and events that are like ourselves and that mirror our own face. The individual who does not want to become a person and responsible, seeks instead to surround himself with images of himself and takes an interest only in whatever promises him a continuation of his selfhood.

Again we can see how this can only go on for a while, as a disability, and during that time we may well be 'on top of the world'. Those around us conspire to preserve us in our state of individualism because they gain from this a vicarious individualism. And why does this individualism appeal so much to us all in any case? Because it demonstrates that humanity is of no account. And why should anyone welcome such a demonstration? Why, simply because in the presence of humanity our wickedness would be exposed. And this wickedness is the great barrier that stands between ourselves and our real benefit.

We say we are not wicked, so naturally we are. By our cowardly sensations we try to continue to persuade ourselves that we are not wicked – and this cowardly sensation is itself wicked.

As soon as we admit we are wicked we can do something about it. Better than that, as soon as we admit to ourselves that we are wicked a stream of humanity begins to influence us, so that gradually our wickedness turns from an activity into a mere liability.

Our cowardly sensations are based, even unconsciously, on the assumption that we are good. We make that assumption as individuals, and it comes naturally to us, because as individuals we are not exposed to the good, only to ourselves and to that and those that are like ourselves, as we choose to experience them. We can get away with such an assumption only until our wickedness has taken its toll, and then cowardice as an inability sets in and we sense only the misery of our state, of our being lonely even in a crowd. Still we do not admit we are wicked, but now we are convinced everyone and everything around us is wicked. We supposed we were victors, now we suspect we are victims. Where before we chose to look at only what we liked, now we cannot help but look at everything we dislike. The disability has become an inability. Our laughter was not true happiness, neither is our weeping now true sorrow. Humanity entered into neither.

76

For the educator, cowardly sensation is of course a crucial issue, because he presents himself to others first of all in terms of experience. He knows that even in regard to the language he uses he may be entirely misunderstood when it comes to his main purpose, which is after all the communication of humanity. What can he do now if he detects in those he is trying to educate an insistence on cowardly sensation? He realizes of course that his reason for being there, within such a pedagogic context, is, precisely, the removal of hindrances to communication, so he does not behave like the standard educator who says: "I will tell you only what you like to hear and what fits in with your various preconceptions." Or maybe he says: "First you have to learn how to hear and see, and then I can educate you." The creative educator makes it his task to hold out to others the real possibility of hearing and seeing, and he knows how difficult his task is, because we, who want to be educated by him, are so far from acknowledging our wickedness that we suppose we are good. Another description or our wickedness, in addition to the moral implications, is that we cannot hear or see the truth. We are blind and deaf to real experience. Any humanity the educator brings our way only stiffens us in our resolve to insist on the world of our own imagining invention. As individuals we are in the habit of making up what suits us, just as a person can make up what suits him, of course, but in the case of a person what he makes up is communal, in the service of others and informed by humanity, but the individual always makes up more replicas of himself. We must think of creativity as lying at the bottom of what the individual does. A person is creative, but the individual's creative urges have been sidetracked and short-circuited. He is self-serving, even in his outwardly most generous-seeming impulses. His altruism, his philanthropy, his evangelism, in short, all his so-called helping is self-serving, and any good he does is accidental and empty of humanity. He may win the Nobel peace prize of be lauded as a saint for all his ameliorative socialism, and yet no humanity was imparted by him, because all he did was alter appearances.

So the educator sees in us not only our unconfessed, unacknowledged wickedness but also our thwarted creativity. He knows that no one can be good and he can tell that we suppose deep down that we are good, and that we confirm ourselves in this error by way of our individualism, by means, in other words, of refusing to sense except what reminds us of our individual self. We have already mentioned how this can mean that we then either form the opinion that all around us are good, like ourselves, which amounts to cowardice as a disability, or else we are persuaded that all around us are bad, once the disability has run it course, whereupon we are stuck in cowardice as an inability. The cowardice prevents us from doing good, and the educator would like us to arrive at that insight.

But how can he expect insight from individuals? A person with insight knows he is wicked, knows he is incapable of a single constructive move while he supposes he is good, and consequently he is able to move away from his ineffectuality and to do good. A person is educated and mature. We are uneducated and immature. We want to be educated and we would like to mature, especially in the company of the educator, who impresses us with something enigmatic that we sense about him, something almost like a power. Perhaps we mistake if for self-assurance. In any case, something about him attracts us, and we are much more likely to seek out his services once our cowardice has passed its pleasant disability stage and become an annoying inability.

If the educator now tells us we are wicked, are we likely to continue to be attracted to him? On the other hand, if he makes his humanity likeable, is it likely to do us good? How is the gap between the educator's individual personality and our impersonal individualism to be bridged?

One attitude widens the gulf, increases the tension and moves resolution beyond the pale. A typical outcome of it is that we agree to call one another good while on earth, especially while we group together under some standard, flag or label, and at the same time we agree to resign ourselves to the impossibility of being 'really good' except on the other side of the grave. The 'really good' is then pictured in glowing colours and fancifully decked out. The creative educator is affronted by such an attitude because he sees it as an enfeebling compromise with cowardice. In direct opposition to it he develops in himself the attitude of a subtle confrontation of wickedness in general combined with an encouragement of creativity in the particular. He says to us: "You are all potentially creative but this wickedness which can get on top of all of us and to which we are all liable prevents you from being creative, hence your dissatisfaction with the world and your wish to be educated and mature rather than timid and immature. But keep in mind that in your fearfulness you are closer to courage then while you suppose you are good. All the same, let me show you a way of being strong and not at all fearful or timid. Let me teach you how to <u>do</u> good. First of all listen to what I am saying to you now and be willing, even glad, to be moved by what I say even if you cannot for the life of you imagine what it might have to do with yourself. Try to listen in such a way that my words become for you entities in themselves. Weigh them against your fearfulness and timidity and notice what happens. You may find that the strength of my words, quite respective of what you would call their meaning, does you good. I say it will do you good

126

to listen to what I say without forming an opinion but always eager to make sense of it. By trying to make sense of what I say you school your senses and by refraining from forming opinions, from saying to yourself: "I think he means this or that," or "What he says reminds me of this or that," you make it possible for your senses to become once again organic after having been for so long mere data processors. Due to your cowardice you have acquired the bad habit of looking and listening so that nothing can inwardly touch or move you. You have acquired a thorough system of looking and listening superficially and trivially. Then every once in a while, to satisfy certain needs, you have bypassed your sense entirely and indulged yourself sensationally, inebriated yourself sensually, so that you let that which is outside or inside you, for which you have now a most uncommon hunger or thirst, touch you in its raw state – indiscriminate, undiscerning, promiscuous. And then, when you noticed what damage this has done you, you resolve in future to sense even more superficially, because you blame your senses, and sensation, and experience, and everything outside and inside you, but quite unjustly, because the fault lies with your ability to sense courageously and strongly. This ability you have lost. If you were not yet an adult I would show you how to do what needs to be done and you would gradually get into the way of it. However since you are an adult, immature and therefore in need of education, I must somehow enlist your freedom of choice in the interest of what you yourself cannot at the moment understand, and that makes my task more interesting but also more difficult. You are 'free' to insist on the judgment of your uprooted, inorganic senses, and you have come to identity such insistence as a strength. You are even proud, at times, of your individualism. That being the case, what hope has a teacher of communicating to you even one morsel of humanity?"

77

The ability to sense courageously and strongly must be learned over a period of time, and a good way to begin is by insisting not on our goodness and on likenesses all around us but on our humanity. Whatever we see or hear we must see or hear in reference to who we are and to whomever we inwardly take ourselves to be at that moment. This is a most interesting exercise and not readily managed right away. An educator or teacher must be familiar with it, else how can he cope with all the cowardice transferred to him? He takes himself aside and says: "Here I am someone. I am the person who has just taken himself aside. I am inordinately conscious of a thousand unpleasant hindrances to my usual good vision and I recognize these for what they are. My task is not to succumb to self-indulgence and sensuality but to overcome this temptation by way of courageous strong vision. As I continue to see and hear, I insist that it is I who see and hear, I who have nothing to fear from an insight into my actual state, since I am not under any delusion of being good. I know I am not good and I have no desire to be good, so I can safely expose myself to the sense experience of the moment, and – I can even go out of my way to insist on such an exposure. I can easily identify the fearfulness, the diffidence that fills me with insecurity. There I exert myself. Where this hateful weakness shows up in me, there, precisely, I sense my environment with a will. There, precisely, my organic sensibility is under attack, is suffering a paralysis, so that a superficial sensibility is to be isolated and divorced. I must above all take hold of my self there and say to it: No! No! You are not going to enfeeble me with this usual masquerade, with this pleasurable veil you like to cast over concrete reality. I insist that I see in terms of myself, in terms of the human being I am, with reference not to what I like but to my humanity. I will se all human gesture and hear all human language as the particular human being I am and not accidentally or promiscuously."

Sometimes it takes just such an exercise for someone to rediscover that he is someone. Notice that any timidity is not veiled or aggravated but employed as a handle, or as a point of leverage. From there sensation is undertaken with a will.

78

We can take this exercise a bit further. At first it is quite likely that our vision will dim somewhat, to the proportion that we have made it mechanical, that we have allowed the organic sense to fall into disuse. There is also a tendency, when we exert ourselves, to exert our muscles instead, and this happens when we mistake a sudden muscular sensation that temporarily accompanies our exerting of ourselves, and then instead of exerting ourselves we indulge in self-exertion, which leads to breakdown by way of wear and tear.

You can begin this exercise by knowing that you are a human being. The point of the exercise is the overcoming of your cowardice. Knowledge is the function of our senses and due to your cowardly sense inability you are not any more in the habit of doing your own knowing. If I say to you: "Know yourself", I mean: Do your own knowing. Use your sense right now organically. Very easily and gently have a go at it. Usually what you know is some passive state of your mind, which activity gives rise to opinions and to counter-opinions, which you then feel duty bound either to defend or else to present tolerantly, whereupon you make a virtue of that tolerance and once again real strength has been bypassed. So do not know a state of your mind but know what goes on all around you. But does that make it necessary that you should lose yourself in your environment? Not at all, because you continually and again make certain that it is you yourself who senses.

This way of organic knowing goes on unhampered in some children and is managed by a few mature adults, but most of

129

the rest of us can benefit greatly from upgrading our capacity for knowing.

Make no attempt to look at anything more closely, to listen to anything more intensely. Eventually your looking and listening will automatically improve. Let your seeing and hearing, and yourself, be the focus of your attention. This or that which you might see or hear (smell and taste and touch follow suit) will present itself in good time or even remove itself in good time. During the course of this exercise you are not to try to see or hear one thing or the other but you are to do your seeing and hearing, of whatever, more specifically and more intentionally yourself. You must do it voluntarily, and you can be much more certain that you are in fact doing it voluntarily and not because someone has told you to do it if you go ahead with it when you don't feel like doing it or when for some unknown reason it seems an absurd or impossible thing to do. Don't forget that your cowardice is not going to take such unfriendly treatment lying down. It will whisper a multitude of reasonable, sensible and prudent objections, and when those don't work it will try to reverse you into some disability so that you should force the issue, violate your body of sense and behave most ungracefully. But again and again you must say to your cowardice: "It is I who decide here, not you. I as the one who I am at this moment see and hear what there is to see and hear, even if it should be a roaring and rushing in my ears or a well of fog in my eyes." Things will adjust themselves and it may seem peculiar. It may seem to you that you begin to 'digest' with your ears and your eyes. You will be less inclined, as time goes on, toe differentiate between the outer and the inner eye. And do not accidentally drift off into semi-consciousness or sleep. If you want to sleet, do so intentionally after you have set an end to your exercise.

130

This book is written for those who want to earn and educate themselves, for those who want to educate other adults and for those who want to teach children. I make no excuse therefore for including in it practical concerns that would be of little interest to anyone outside these three groups.

The exercise we have just begun to look at serves to rid us equally of cowardly and arrogant sensation. When we feel overbearing and unlimited, or when we feel, or rather when we are – timid and fearful, then is a good time to begin with such an exercise because the place where we are, in ourselves, fearful or overbearing, is also the place where we can most successfully draw on our humanity. But we do not have to wait until we are actually conscious of being at that moment arrogant or cowardly in terms of our sensation. We can take it for granted that there exists in us a backlog of material – a mountain, shall we say – that has accumulated due to our arrogance and cowardice in the past, and that due to this barrier we are forced to – or tend to – sense superficially at one time and be sensual at another. These two should not exist. That barrier should be removed, this wedge that splits our organic sensation. A multitude of teachings, pseudo-scientific, artificial, 'religious', exist to justify this wedge, to perpetuate the existence of it, as though, since once we had begun to wear blinkers, we must from then on explain the world as narrow.

Organic sensation is a distinct possibility for all, but an absolute necessity for those who would educate or teach.

79

Before the teacher can encourage organic sensation in his pupils he must be capable of it himself. He must be aware of his seeing and hearing. He must be able to see and hear in awareness, and it must be he himself who does the seeing and hearing and not his eyes and ears. Let him practice <u>organic vision</u>. Let him take himself to task about his inability to see and hear with his whole organic being. Is he even aware of

131

being whole organically? Can he tell the difference between his organic integrity and a disturbance of it? If not, then he has no business standing in front of children promising them maturity –

– because maturity means an organically intact body, just as adulthood implies an ability, if not a willingness, to always again become organically intact. If these are just words for a teacher he is not really a teacher at all but very likely an immature adult who is passing on his own brand of immaturity.

An organically intact body is sense knowledge ready for communication. Such sense knowledge, and such a body, comes from using our own eyes and ears and then not forming judgments but simply remembering. What we take in like this cannot but stay with us. And still always we will wonder why we cannot reproduce it at will. But we can. Whatever we fully remember stays with us as knowledge for all time. If we make wrong demands on our nature we are mercifully frustrated. Organic sensation is a just demand on our nature. It lovingly includes appearances but does not depend on them. We come up against the twin barrier of arrogance and cowardice in ourselves either during an exercise of organic sensation or else when we communicate, or try to communicate, our knowledge. A teacher has certain knowledge, organic knowledge, and he tries to communicate it as he draws on his humanity and not on a backlog of memorized data. Such data are pretexts for him.

Someone who plays a musical instrument in the company of others, for example, does so, if he knows what he is about, so as to communicate his certain knowledge. There is an educator in the serious musician, in the dramatic actor, in the playwright. We either pander to one another's arrogance and cowardice or we communicate our knowledge.

As the teacher in the classroom communicates his knowledge, he wants his pupils to hear and see, to learn how to hear and see. He wants to come to the point, eventually, where they are capable of sense knowledge, of bodily vision that is organic. What happens is that his pupils automatically transfer their cowardice to him. They cannot help but do that if they are to take him at his word when he says: "Here is my knowledge," and he offers what he has. The pupils do not realize that they transfer their cowardice to the teacher. They have acquired bad habits of sensation and these clash with what the teacher offers, so they relinquish them, and the teacher senses them in himself. A lassitude overcomes him, and an anger at not being able to cope. He loses courage. It cannot be otherwise. Now he must take care not to react against this loss of courage in himself. As soon as we lose courage we tend to strike back. It takes most courage of all to turn the other cheek. And the teacher is able to tell that his knowledge is being attempted by his pupils as soon as this lassitude, or a kind of sour mood, steals over him. This is cowardice as inability. He feels like throwing in the towel, he feels like letting himself rage to frighten them. He wants to pick holes in their behaviour, to complain of their discipline.

We have moved on from sensation to feeling. Cowardly sensation the teacher experiences as an insistence on mere appearances. He will find himself wanting to see his pupils seated and quiet, looking obedient. He will tend to concentrate on superficial details in the classroom. Whatever the form or content of the work, let is be neat and tidy. He will notice himself becoming superficial, and this will tell him that he has an opportunity now to educate his pupils specifically in terms of courageous organic sensation. There is a very specific experience which the teacher finds himself undergoing in the company of pupils whose sensation is spoiled by mass media exposure. His sensitivity to all around him will seem impaired, he seems dull and callous and tends to sudden outbursts of lost temper. He will in fact notice how

133

again and again he completely ignores precisely this function of himself as a conductor of negative energies, as a transformer of such energies into strength and freedom. The effect on him is the same as the effect on his pupils, and typically he loses track of the fact that this is so. Mass media cultures put paid to all education of the senses. That is what one would expect and it seems to be happening. Where the mass media are employed even in the classroom, this unfortunate process of sense-alienation is sped up. Only where this tragic divorce of the senses from emotion and feeling is already fairly complete do these media actually seem to enliven the pupils, because here the mere senses are stimulated while emotion and feeling is not any more under threat because dead. It is hard to believe what adults do to children once their own sensitivity to life has disappeared; has been killed off.

Where the senses are not supported and substantiated by emotion and feeling they process data, so that the demonic element is at liberty to move in and hold sway. But it is equally true that emotion and feeling must be nourished and nursed by sensation. This is the Jacob's ladder, on which the angels travel up and down. We are not much accustomed to viewing emotion, feeling and sense as one single continuum. A mature human being has a body which means just that. Let's put it this way: There is a discontinuity between a mature human being and reality thanks to that human being's body as emotion, feeling and sense. Due to all the disruptions in our body, of feeling, sense and emotion from one another, we do well to come to some clear understanding of how our body is in truth constituted. The old model of body and soul has nothing to do with this. It was in fact invented to comfort us while we were still not receptive to the creative spirit in person. Now the issue of that spirit is pressing, and with regard to it our soul is visible as our mind or invisible as our body, while that which was usually called our body is revealed as our flesh.

80

A great deal needs to be said about the education of our senses, or of us in terms of our senses, outwardly to world and inwardly to emotion and feeling.

We see the light of day which illumines even the darkness. Children must be educated to see the light of day; on their own they cannot manage it. Teachers have their work cut out for them here. As the child becomes a pupil his inwardness must at once be called on, for here the teacher, by means of his own inwardness, has immediate access. If he were to rely on any sensible means of communication he would just not be seen or heard, for he can take it for granted that the senses of these children are worn out by habit. Where children are accustomed and addicted to mass media, they will not tolerate any other medium. Any live medium, such as human language, grates on their nerves or leaves them befuddled. The choice left to the teacher is the insensible medium of his own feeling and emotion, so that in a way he undercuts the spoiled senses of the pupils.

Now we have to ask what it is that goes on in the teacher's realm of emotion and feeling when first he confronts such pupils. While his own senses are revolted, his emotion and feeling remains untouched, remains entirely his own. What he does here is therefore spontaneous. But cowardice is transferred to him as soon as he behaves spontaneously, because then the pupils are inwardly touched, so that they ignore their senses and feel, right away off-loading on the teacher their inhibited and repressed emotion. All this time the teacher has perhaps not opened his mouth. Spontaneous behaviour does not require speech. He has done nothing which he intended to be significant or meaningful. His entire concentration was expended on his inwardness of emotion and feeling, where he was entirely himself, and of course superbly ready for that transfer of cowardice to himself whenever it should come. And come it will, because the pupils, in the absence of any sensible medium against which to rebel, are super-responsive in terms of emotion and feeling. Neither do they, of course, need to say anything in order for the transfer of feelings and emotions to take place. A casual onlooker would notice the teacher walking into the classroom, hanging up his coat, arranging a few objects on his desk, while the pupils are occupied in various ways, in small groups or singly. The teacher is thoroughly aware of what he is about and gradually the children become more aware of his presence and of him. Five or ten minutes might be taken up like this towards the beginning of a period. Of course the teacher might casually chat with some of the pupils, comment on their appearance, greet them by name, but all of this would occur to him spontaneously or not at all, because that is his pedagogic approach within the present context, for the specific purpose of bypassing the trivialized sensibilities of his pupils. He is making body contact with his pupils, but entirely in terms of feeling and emotion, his own being spontaneous and visible to the pupils as his behaviour, and theirs being equally spontaneous in response to his, while they at the same time transfer feelings and emotions – or rather while this happens, since the children do not, after all, do this intentionally or consciously.

81

What we take note of here is that while the teacher is superbly aware of his inward emotion and feeling, which expresses itself spontaneously as his behaviour, the children are not at all aware of their inward emotion and feeling. We can therefore with justice speak of the <u>live art</u> of the teacher. It is the art not of an artist, but more than that. It is the art of an art-worker, who creates in himself first of all the preconditions for the work eventually to be achieved. To the casual

onlooker what he does in the classroom is without signifi-
cance, but his behaviour among his pupils is spontaneous and
therefore immediately effective, making it possible for them
to relate to him insensibly and to respond to him emotionally
and with feeling. Such a response must come as a surprise to
those children themselves because they have for some time
had no true inwardness. Remember that their senses have, as
it were, become detached from feeling and emotion.

82

Cowardly feeling, first as a pleasurable disability, allows
us to renounce all responsibility for how we make contact
with those around us. We do in fact aim for irresponsible
contact, and while we succeed in this we are gradually
drained of all energy.

Contact is responsible while we keep in mind the autonomous being of the one in relation with us. This autonomous
being is actual or potential, or only assumed. But we must keep
it in mind if the way we feel is not to become promiscuous.

But this promiscuity feels great. It makes us feel really
alive – though it is all a sham. It is as if the bounds of our
body were being destroyed, while we suppose ourselves to be
at liberty. But the bounds and limits of our body are extremely important. Knowledge is impossible except in a
measured way. What we feel must be felt in the awareness of
the fact that we feel, otherwise we undergo an adultery of our
human being. Our own autonomous human being is the most
precious possession we have, and when it becomes adulter-
ated there is cause for concern.

Bodily contact, by way of feeling, or what we might call
felt experience, must be understood aright before we can get
a useful notion of the various aberrations of it that set in.

The crucial experience is tact. The knowledge we feel is
the tact of a being. It is the tact of that being in that time at
that place and we can learn to make allowances for it by get-

ting into the way of appreciating our own tact. It has to do with stimulus and response, with impulse, inertia and momentum. To be aware of this can be in itself a major task, especially if we have behaved promiscuously and adulterously, feeling but not responsible for what we feel, ignoring the autonomous being of the person or thing whose being we feel.

There is the tact of someone's being, and there is the tact of my own being, and with this notion of tact we must acquaint ourselves.

83

The tact we mean is contemporary. In other words, to feel it I need the sense and emotion of that being at the same time. One has to be left to it entirely and wholly. No contact without tact. We speak of being inwardly touched by something or by someone. That plays into what we mean by tact. It is the present aliveness of a being, not to this or to that, but in itself. In a poem, and in language in general, we speak of cadence, meaning the fall of the voice, the equal proportion of movement.

To be in touch means to have tact; but in touch with what? It means inwardly in touch. It means a gathered collectedness of inward sensibility and spirit. When someone is tactless in manner he leaves out of consideration that inward being of another.

Tact, then, is felt inward being. We must first have it in ourselves, and then we can assume it, even posit it, in another being. Its being contemporary is of crucial importance, because as soon as we lose tack of the fact that our inward being does not exist for the sake of other beings, in communion with us, we mistake it for a feeling of heightened aliveness, of pleasurable intensity, and then, due to this disabling pleasure, we tend to augment the aliveness as mere feeling, and we want to intensify the pleasure, naturally, though not human-naturally, and usually we do this not only because this bastard pleasure is magically attractive but also because it promises us a relief from dread and from the risk of exposure. We cower before an enemy and it feels good to cower. It begins to feel downright pious and holy. We justify the feeling and become sanctimonious. To us, of course, it seems saintly. In fact we inwardly consume ourselves. Compare the consumptive lifestyle of the so-called romantic artist, who stands as a visible symptom of the invisible inward corruption of his society. An immorality, a hollowness of character sets in. Still this feeling of advanced self-righteousness may be vigorously pursued. It does not occur to us how selfishly we cling to the impulses from our human nature that are available to us so that we should communicate them. We stimulate one another in this aberration, psychically, to increase the pleasure even more, and come up with cults of feeling, in our attempts to make the pleasure institutionally repeatable and permanent. Human-natural instincts for communion are cultivated in isolation and thereby perverted and abused. Again, the aim is a pleasure to replace a dread.

We do well to ask: Whence the dread? Because as soon as we even begin to cultivate our inward being for ourselves alone we are right away coaxed, by outward circumstances, not to do this, and then we suppose we must protect ourselves against these 'attacks'. The coaxing turns into demand, the demand into persecution. Do we take the persecution for a sign that we are special, and do we intensify the perverse pleasure of our stunted inwardness even more, espousing isolation from those who are 'getting at us', and from the thing we suppose is making us feel pain, even from the elements? Or do we 'pray for those who persecute us'?

We can see here how the decision and practice to wish those well whose effect and influence on us we experience with dread and dismay amounts to a powerful and successful overcoming of our cowardice because it constitutes a violent communion.

Human feeling is body contact with the inner being of others. It is that kind of knowledge, compared, for example, to sense knowledge, or human sense. We may assume the tact of all other beings, and equally we assume the tact of our own being. The reason we do this is so that we have something to work with. We are not talking about feelings, which are at best raw material, but about a way of knowing, which is voluntary, intentional and conscious. In order to know, we have to come out of our selves and move towards others. Where this communal move is not made, cowardice sets in.

Either we recognize the onset of cowardice and overcome it, in spite of the pleasure it involves, or we become more and more attached to its dysfunctional aspects. The disability then grows on us, and we stop growing in that area of our being. Impulses of human-natural feeling are short-circuited, we become fond of ourselves and mistake it for something like a fondness of god for us. Religiosity is mistaken for religion. We feel good and so we suppose we must be good. For contact with others we substitute party feeling and crowd appeal. The illusion of human warmth is taken for the real thing. An immaculate inwardness turns into an efflorescence of worthlessness, while many are attracted to us on account of this falsehood. They are our fans. They delight in our popularity. They too desire the dysfunctional pleasure with which we are endowed and which radiates from us as charisma. When our feelings are burnt out they will flee from us, as parasites flee from the unfortunate host. But for the time being, when disability has not yet flipped over into inability, they cling to us for the poor pleasure that gives them, because it rubs off on them.

The dismay sets in when we feel that our luck is deserting us. It is amazing how much so-called good luck was merely an accumulation of tactless feeling.

To be tactful – to have contact with another soul: if we persevere in this we will gradually come away with a wholly new approach to everything and everyone around us. We may have lost entirely the capacity for real feeling. Perhaps we have got out of the habit of paying attention. Our body needs to be built up. We are familiar only with feelings, so-called good ones and bad ones, meaning pleasant and unpleasant – meaning disability and inability. So true or real feeling, being tactful, at first must seem like nothing to us, because it is nothing compared to feelings. Then we learn that feelings are nothing compared to feeling, and so we pay better attention to this invisible aspect of our soul, which is our body, and to this tactful part of our body, which is feeling. Feelings are what we get when we try to sense our own body, but then we have neither sense nor feeling but a kind of self-consumption.

The best way to commence with real feeling is to let it support our sensing. What we see and hear out here is also felt. We do not say: "What does it feel like to be looking into someone's eyes or at a table spread with food?" but we see, and support what we see with our feeling. We feel what we see. This should be called perception. To perceive means to feel and see at the same time. We cannot any more rely on this happening without our conscious effort. The effort will have to become good habit. We must learn to perceive.

The teacher, who knows how to perceive, looks at his pupils and detects the beginnings of unsupported sense. Most of all he pays attention to any number of feelings that happen to the children, like accidents. He does not mistake 'good' feelings for feeling, or for anything worthwhile. Nor is he dismayed by bad feeling. In fact he sets himself the task of countermanding both by insisting, in himself, on real feeling. An artistic teacher might fall into the trap of rejecting dismay, 'bad' feelings, in favour of a nonsensical distraction, but a creative teacher sees through the veil of both. A pupil might seem all sweetness and light, but the creative teacher looks for something solid, something that will not collapse under the weight of misfortune. He brings his own tactful feeling into play emphatically and then he can tell right away if the ground there is hollow, so that he perseveres, patiently assuming even the possibility of tactful being in that pupil. And he behaves in the same way if the disability in the pupil has become inability, unpleasant feelings, such as boredom, a sour disapproval, an embittered sensibility, or even wrathfulness. He is not dismayed by the dismay of his pupils but he cuts through it with his own tactful being, which is feeling in support of sense.

86

Once the teacher becomes adept at bringing his tactful body-knowledge into play, he responds almost automatically to dismay or to disgrace with solid perception, which includes sound sense and fine feeling. However, this perception cannot be spontaneous unless substantiated by emotion.

Disgrace is what we call the disability of feeling, and this gives us a clue to how substantial fine feeling must be, since it involves grace and opens all possibility. Dismay is the closure of possibility, while disgrace is the forfeiture of grace.

So inability of feeling signals itself in a pupil when he is more persuaded by what he cannot do than he is impressed by what he can do. He becomes languid and unwilling, he is despondent, later on he becomes pessimistic, cynical and sarcastic. Various afflictions of the flesh play into this.

87

Sometimes the teacher will assert himself in front of a pupil, only to discover that this has no effect whatsoever. The pupil exists in a world of his own and will not be moved. A hardening of feeling has set in, and the teacher's first impulse will be to give the pupil a good shake, to make him aware, by force, of himself the teacher, so that communication can proceed. But if the pupil gets frightened, no feeling is discovered. The teacher must overcome the feeling of frustration in himself. It has been transferred to him from the pupil and he has to make an end of it in himself.

All the cowardly feelings are transferred to the teacher and he has to make an end of them in himself. They are not his own feelings, but he must deal with them as though they were. All the same, let him keep in mind that they are not his own. This awareness is a pedagogic necessity to which we continue to refer because we forget it so often. These cowardly feelings, such as rushing off or flying off the handle, must be kept in perspective, otherwise they cannot be handled. And by knowing they are not his own, the teacher does keep them in perspective. One of the worst afflictions for a teacher can be this recognition of dead feeling in a pupil. It seems to him that nothing can be done. But of course the most important thing in this realm can be done, which might be called a resurrection of feeling.

The cowardice we mean here, like the arrogance we mentioned earlier, is not a moral issue but a spiritual one, and therefore also an affliction of the flesh. Spirit is incarnate, just like flesh is inspired. We have all our mythological faculties, to comfort us when we cannot tell that spirit is incarnate and when we doubt that flesh is inspired, and the art practice by the creative teacher makes use of it. He knows it, when art becomes a part of his creativity. It is not artistry, he is not being artistic. His art subserves his creativity. That is why we take care to call it creative art, as distinct from the product of the artist, which is limited by the social sphere and knows nothing of communality.

A creative teacher makes an actual decision to avail himself of art under certain given circumstances, and dead feeling, which then of course also means dead sense and dead emotion, is such an occasion, when the teacher at first will feel inclined to throw in the towel. Then he realizes that now has come the time for his creativity to become artful. He brings to mind that all things are possible to him who believes that they are, and he remembers that the good is not forced or earned or contracted by us, but given to us, gracefully.

Creative art springs from those two certainties.

88

Not that creative art goes beyond creativity but it is an extension of it, under special circumstances. Now while the supreme act of cowardice is a running away from death, in whatever category of our existence, this work of creative art is like a supreme act of faith. We can not any longer depend on our own efforts, such as an acquired habit of creativity, where one thing leads to the next as we rely on, say, intuition or instinct, or make use of intelligence and intellect, but we must allow ourselves once again to be acted upon, directly, becoming totally placid and pacific, but in a spirit of ultimate readiness and in the knowledge that we ourselves are about to be changed. Our work will be a simple registration of that, and we ourselves will not know anything about it. All we can know at the time is the fact of the achievement.

So the teacher invents, and he brings especially his fantasy into play. Now he makes contact with ease and with the unexpected.

89

Impossible to imagine the teacher as separate from his pupils during such an artful process. Something special goes on, and we who stand outside this process at the moment cannot comprehend what goes on. First we ourselves would have to participate in the crucial movement here, which is the giving up of our individuality for that of another, or the submission of our individuality to that of another.

144

Because the teacher's sole concern is that the pupil should confront his dead feeling-capacity and not run away. It seems incredible that this should be possible. Would the child not much rather continue in a state of painless deadness if any change at all necessarily involves pain? The teacher himself experiences this deadness in himself now, transferred to him, and himself would run away, and yet he contains it, knowledgably, within the pedagogic perspective. Outwardly nothing goes on, but inwardly here is stress and tension. And the teacher may take it as given that the child does not experience this stress and tension because he, the teacher, does. All depends now on how the teacher behaves under this burden of transferred tension and stress. His entire body, emotion, feeling and sense, is affected by it and all that prevents him from condemning the child, outwardly or inwardly, is his conscious awareness of the fact that things are indeed as we have here described them.

Nothing that he does now may interfere with this conscious awareness. We spoke of ease and grace, of fantasy and invention. In terms of these now the teacher addresses himself to the child. None of these, if he adheres to them, will interfere with his pedagogic awareness. The stress and tension remains a contained matter for him. He makes no reference at all to it, not even within himself, where in truth it is actually gradually being 'digested' and absorbed, while he – speaks to the child.

It is precisely in speech now, and as speech, that grace and fantasy come into play. The teacher does not talk but he speaks. In talk there is always an element of confession, usually unconscious confessions, where, without knowing that we do it, we transfer to another our shortcomings and inhibitions in the hope that he will respond creatively, that is to say, in such a case as this, in a manner to at least reassure, if not to mend or heal. We talk to one another, hoping for compassion, though of course not at all necessarily on the conscious level. So while it makes sense that an adult should talk to a child, since children are remarkably capable of human compassion, it also makes sense that under the circumstances described above, the teacher should <u>not</u> talk to the vulnerable child, but that this is a time for speech, so that the teacher's own masterful creativity is displayed to the child, over a period of time.

We find out more about this speech in comparison to talk if we describe it as artful. Remember now, not artistic but artful; not drawing somehow on the child's present state of being around, on the way the child affects us, how he appeals to us or rejects us, but relying entirely on the way we ourselves are, as human beings, and drawing on our human being. Speech derives from personal integrity, from an honourable attitude towards any human being, from a persuasion of owing that other one, however he affects us, capable respect and a lively responsibility.

We don't usually think of honour, integrity, duty, respect, responsibility 'in the same breath' with grace, ease, pleasure, fantasy and invention, but here in this case of artful creativity as speech, this is precisely what we have. It sounds ever so complicated but happens to be the simplest thing in the world. The pleasure is a thing that may come to the teacher himself as a surprise the first few times.

But it does need to be emphasized that a careful and circumspect study needs to be undertaken of this artful creativity as a preparation for it, precisely because it is such a specialty and so that it can in fact go on and be done on the spot and at the required time – spontaneously.

90

It cannot be called an artful approach. As an approach to the pupil, to the one who is to mature and, specifically in this case, whose bodily function of feeling is to be revived, it

146

would be artistic, not artful, and it would have to fail, because at best the child would be momentarily relieved of the dead weight which his feeling, and his body, has become. During any artistic approach in such a case the teacher does not take upon himself the child's predicament in the first place; he is not aware that a transfer of sense, emotion or feeling has taken place and he treats his own experience as disconnected from any experience of the child. At the same time the child is observed by him at a distance, and an art product of some sort is employed by him as a medium. Even his artistic talk may serve as such an art-productive medium. The idea is, that the child should be stimulated, pacified, etc. And this is to go on in line with some idea in the educator's head. Every artist works with ideas, consequently no fundamental change comes about, but a change in manner, in contingency, in outward manifestation, while the inward state remains the same.

Artful creativity is not an approach to the child, via a medium, but something is done for the child which he cannot do for himself, and it is done in such a way that the child will in fact experience within himself a resurrection of the body as his body. How this manifests outwardly at the time is unpredictable and the experienced creative teacher pays no heed to it. He is not put off if the pupil would momentarily seem to turn against him. This would only mean that the child is so preoccupied with this new inward experience that he cannot help but give his entire attention to it. At a standard school the conventional responses always carry the day. Even where artistic education finds its way into such a school, the work will always be geared towards a 'show' of convention, which is not a mere show, but something that all the same leaves the inward child untouched.

The artful speech, of the teacher may seem to him, at the time, superfluous, while he is still impressed by the effect of deadness transferred to himself. He supposes he can hold out against the pupil, because he mistakes the deadness in himself, characteristically, as an invulnerability. The pupil may be making all kinds of demands on him, that seem preposterous, outrageous, illogical and unjust and it will seem to the teacher that his own best 'defence' is to remain sensible, controlled and generally aloof from such nonsense. However, while he defends himself he is not doing the child any good. And the pupil will generally persist. If the teacher does not behave creatively he will continue to use the feeling of deadness transferred to him as though it were a shield, only to have to realize how suddenly it is pierced, leaving him outraged.

So how is the teacher to find his way from the experience of dead feeling and a dead body to the utterance of artful speech?

First, of course, he must realize that the deadness has been transferred to him and he must practice an awareness of this, sufficiently, for the sake of the pedagogic perspective, which is also an ordinary human perspective. If he loses that perspective he becomes either frightened or demonic, and usually one leads to the other. So he must know what he is doing and not lie down on the job.

And out of this awareness is born the spontaneous, artful speech. A sufficiency of perspective awareness suddenly becomes speech, which the teacher is free, perfectly free, to utter or not to utter. He recognizes it by this freedom. It is not a speech into which he is seduced by circumstances. It does not come over him, or upon him. He remains completely at liberty to speak or not to speak, and his decision to speak rather than to remain silent will hinge solely on his wish to educate the child. He wants to do the child the good that he has come here to do.

91

Finally, on this topic of 'free speech that raises the dead', we are bound to discover that cowardly emotion, like cowardly feeling, is not in need of excuses but of being purged. Where cowardly emotion has settled in and formed like a pool of like-warm evasiveness in ourselves we soon seem to lack even the wherewithal for differentiating between cowardice and courage. Because emotion is basic. If emotion came down to a few shallow sentiments we would soon be done with it. But it dictates a great many things that depend on it. Honesty, for example. In order to be able to see and say things as they are we must be capable of a solidarity of emotion. Can we rest in ourselves in the knowledge of peace? Is our spirit of such a temper that in contact with our emotion it spends and expends peace, so that others have the use of it, or does it work itself up into a turmoil because we tend to become emotional?

For a teacher to mistake the content of emotion amounts to a grave fault. The immature adult in search of education must be continually reassured of the possibility of real inward peace or he will not dare leave the stronghold of his delusions. A child has emotion that is never quite up to the demands made on it by immature adults, so the risk of distortion always exists, but peace can mend it.

So the cause of shaky emotion is a lack of peace, and such peace must be supplied by the educator, both to the immature adult and to the child.

Now it would seem simple enough to suggest that the teacher who is peaceful in himself automatically works peace outwardly, and of course there is truth in that; but it doesn't help us, who wish to educate, to maintain and regain our peace when we are being assailed by cowardly emotions. Even given that we are fairly free of laying blame and accusing when the ground in us trembles, we are still not at all necessarily in the know about how to lay strong inward foundations so as to be able to step in front of others and say: "Let loose your emotions on me, for I will translate them for you, into solid emotion." And yet an educator should be able to say that. And if he cannot see it through with a degree of success he needs to return to basics, that is, to his own ground of emotion, to test for hollowness and to lay in support. The maturing spirit cannot operate through him if his own soul, as body, is readily undermined. Where a pupil feels tempted to exercise foolishness in confrontation with a teacher, that teacher may himself be the temptation, if he has approached his pupil on thin ice.

92

We can probe our own emotion. The ability and the willingness to do so would seem almost indispensible to an educator, since he cannot know ahead of time what sort of emotions are going to be fired at him during the course of his work. So, during times of peace when he is on his own he does well to test the ground in himself, and there is no better way than a work of art, either created or recreated.

Or let's right away be mindful of the distinction we made earlier, and speak specifically of art-works, to exclude those works of art which appeal to our social ego but do not nourish or advance our communality. Only an art-work, when creativity has aided itself with art, can be both created and recreated, so that it would amount to the same, for someone who wishes to probe his emotion, whether he composes a, say, poetic artwork himself or avails himself of one composed by another. The word recreation would take care of both aspects, since the teacher who would do such a work himself would of course be doing it primarily for his own purpose.

So where our purpose is the testing of our emotion, and of the solidity of our ground of emotion, we gain that purpose through something we call recreation, and hopefully this will not get confused with the popular meaning, which often stands for types of self-indulgence.

150

By recreation, then, we mean first of all an exercising of present emotion, which may involve an exorcising of emotions.

*

I present the following as an example of what I mean:

> The emptiness within me,
> Where once spirits caroused
> Untroubled by earth and world,
> Trembles upon contact with love,
> Whereupon I make my peace.
>
> The fullness within me
> Perpetuates a warm light
> Lingering upon landscape,
> A sensed memory of youth
> Constantly within reach.
>
> These swings of the pendulum
> Keep me in tact with my
> Human ancestry in god
> And I do make allowances
> For significant breakthroughs.

I call this a recreation for myself because my emotion was enlisted, brought to the fore and confirmed. During this process several emotions were eliminated. You yourself can use that poem to the same end. But if you do, you need to be aware all the time of why you are doing it, or you will be reading it for understanding alone, perhaps, or for some other reason. My own understanding of it can be managed another time. What counts solely is that emotion wins out against emotions, first and then equally against feelings and sensations. Emotion will always readily manifest itself as language, and any language that is understandable to others will do. A secret language will not do, because then emotion is short-changed or short circuited.

93

Cowardly emotion occurs as a disability in the following way. An appeal is made to our emotion and we come out with emotions instead, becoming emotional, either to the point or not, and taking pleasure in the way this warms our blood and blinds us to our self. If someone were to tell us not to be emotional we would seriously question his right to do so. We hold forth and are full of ourselves and no one should get in our way. Most commonly our feelings and sensations are brought into it too, and then we consider ourselves to be passionate. We may even fly into a passion, which means that we have become quite careless of our body and heedless of the body of others. We enjoy, at any rate, being the centre of attention, little realizing the vanity of that enjoyment.

An emotional disability on its own is not easy to identify because it may be cloaked by a mere routine of sense and feeling. An educator would, however, set himself the task of learning to identify it, not out there, but as transferred to himself. He would then translate it into emotion and present it to the pupil as language. We will speak of this translation of emotions into emotion after we have dealt with emotional inability.

94

The emotional disability links us pleasurably to one another in a way that bypasses our humanity and literally empties us of life. Emotion differs from feeling in that we are open to good spirit but not yet to one another. When we open to one another's high spirits but not to good spirit we are involved in emotional disability.

Many adults are not aware of good spirit even as a probability, and in their case an education would have to start from simple information about such spirit. One would have to acquaint them first of all with good spirit in action so that they may confront their emotional immaturity and their lack of emotion, their lack of a substantial body. If that has not yet happened, such adults are forever looking in a wrong direction for satisfaction and they seem to themselves to come close, but then the prize is snatched away again, not because they really did come close but because they had the wrong prize in mind. Children, by comparison, are not yet intent on fastening their will and intellect to side issues, so that even if most of their experience has been devoid of good spirit, they respond much more readily than adults to an instance of it. On the other hand, once an adult knows that good spirit exists and is probable, he has what it takes to do the probing so that he can then emotionally recreate himself. The child requires the example and direction of the teacher.

But adults in any case are not often interested in good spirit once they have discovered spirit, because they draw energy from spirit, they look for inspiration and generally open themselves to a world of troubles and woes without realizing it at the time. If one could explain to adults the risks they take when they court indiscriminate spirit and the benefits they miss by not taking on board that good spirit as such exists, and that it exists for them, one might make some headway. But indifferent spirit is such a dramatic change from deadness, dullness and dross that we jump at the chance of an interesting revival without first making certain that the experience is solidly based.

A few pointers can be given here. Good spirit is peacefully incarnate, while indifferent, indiscriminate spirit is not. Good spirit is not to be distinguished as in any way separate from live flesh. Every human being eventually bears witness to this. From the point of view of real human being, which can equally be called divine being, reality is spirit or flesh, depending on how we look at it. But then we mean good spirit and live flesh, not indifferent spirit and corrupt flesh. Reconciliation and atonement are words usually used to describe what has been done here, and what we can do ourselves by leaning on this accomplished fact.

95

Incarnate spirit and inspired flesh are one and the same. We might have to overcome a few premature judgments in ourselves before we can grasp that. We have a long tradition behind us of viewing all flesh as corrupt and our actions have been such as if we were intent on confirming that view. But as we believe, so it is unto us.

In the interest of our proximity to incarnate good spirit and inspired live flesh we are pleased to learn that just as the former is probable, in that it may be tested and proved to be good, so is the latter palpable, in that it may be touched and handled. What we test and what we handle is one an the same.

We also have a long tradition behind us of viewing spirit as detached from flesh, almost as though we were afraid that all spirit might also be bad, depending on its arbitrary will. So we do well to differentiate between good spirit, or god, and indifferent, indiscriminate spirit, which need not concern us.

96

We can see more clearly now in which direction fundamental emotion is to be sought. How can anyone teach who cannot distinguish between fundamental emotion and emotions? Emotions either disable us or we are unable because of them. Since maturity implies good effectiveness, the teacher will see it as a priority that those he teaches should learn to distinguish between emotion and emotions, so that they might choose the former and not be diverted by the latter. The same goes for passion and passions. We see passion as emotion, feeling and sense all in one. If it matters to us that passion should work for us we need to know of the incarnate good spirit and of the inspired live flesh, and we need to perceive that these two are one and the same, otherwise we will always again be separated in ourselves, drawn one way by

154

indifferent spirit, which inspires indiscriminately, and the other way by corrupt flesh, which pleases monstrously.

Where emotion has become a disability, as pleasurable emotions and emotionality, the teacher must, in a sense, wait until that false liveliness has settled, and by waiting he can do the best work. This is much better than to prevent, to chastise, to preach doom. Of course the teacher cannot close his eyes to the fact that the inability will succeed the disability, and that pain will take the place of the pleasure. But he also knows that nothing can be changed by external intervention, such as apprehensiveness would dictate. If and when he knows the apprehensiveness in himself, which is always after the manner of: "Now they laugh, but then they will weep", he must translate it, in himself, into fundamental emotion by understanding: "This is the time when the roots go deeper in me, when the foundation becomes stronger in me, when my nerve system becomes more stable. And as this which I do goes on in me I am setting the best possible example for those who would learn from me. I am showing by my inward behaviour and conduct that burn-out and break-down are not unavoidable consequences of emotion on the loose as emotions. I am demonstrating that these straying pieces of myself can be gathered in like a harvest, and those who would learn from me will be inspired and pleased to follow suit."

97

What does it mean, to translate, in myself, emotions into emotion? This is easy to say and to repeat, but not necessarily something we have ever done consciously. We tend to play along with pleasurable emotions and to repress painful ones, and that is in fact a standard way of inward behaviour and of doing what we suppose, even on reflection, is worth doing.

However we have learned now that emotions, like feelings and sensations, all of which can be summed up as passions, are not creative, and not conducive to life. We are not to detect them in others, but in ourselves. This shuts out criticism and condemnation of others. Besides, passions are not bad, only not good, so if we are to look upon them correctly as raw-materials we have no business resisting them. Still, the pain and pleasure of them in ourselves, whether they begin in us or are transferred to us, sway us in their favour or disfavour, and so we need to make use of our adult faculty of abstraction in order to obtain material we can manage instead of being swayed by it.

Now take a cowardly disability emotion such as piousness (as distinct from piety). Here we are willing to indulge ourselves pleasurably in our own being good, and we find it attractive that so much of our inwardness should be approved by us, on account of various virtues which we discover afterwards, out of the blue, so as to sustain that grateful pleasure at being good. The hollowness of the emotion 'causes' us to underpin it with evidence, to surround it with standards and to colour it as realistically as possible. It does not feel great, to be so good. I want to make the point that we are not dealing with a feeling here. Emotions need to be individually identified, especially by a teacher, who offers himself as a carrier of the emotions of others.

I like myself when I am good and because I am not entirely secure in my goodness I produce proof of it. Notice, I produce proof not from joy but from fear. This is what will burn me out eventually. Piousness, as a cowardly disability emotion, will eventually let me down precisely because I load it more and more heavily with signs. These signs are to fool me and others, but my mature human being insists on truth and must therefore let me know somehow that I am out on a limb, or rather that I am consuming substance with which I should be building.

As soon as I notice what is going on, anywhere along the road to the crisis or at the point of crisis itself, I can switch

156

over to human being. I can say: "This is not really myself I am promulgating but some aspect of my self." I will then experience shame. This lets me know that now I am on the right track. Shame is an experience that sets in in the case of all the cowardly passions, and in the case of this piousness it overcomes – or convicts – me as soon as I stop indulging myself in self approval. The translation of the emotion piousness into emotion, piety, succeeds as soon as I accept this shame and let it do its work. If I fly into the face of it, by defending myself or by justifying my piousness, I harden in my error.

So a readiness for shame is ultimately of crucial importance. Due to this readiness I recognize as soon as possible the error of my ways, such as in this present case the supposition that I might be good and still human.

98

We can generalize at this point and emphasize the crucial importance of shame and guilt, and of our readiness and openness to these. Guilt is the sign that presently our arrogant passions, or an arrogant passion, is being changed into passion, while shame is the evidence we have that a cowardly passion is being changed in us into passion.

The openness to guilt is called humility and the readiness for shame is called courage.

Now it ever we are not sufficiently open to guilt, that is to say, if we are not humble enough on some occasion, we actually experience guilt, and then it is important for us to know that we are fortunate that we are able to experience it, because our arrogance is just then being changed into humility. And equally if we are not courageous enough on some occasion we can be glad that we experience shame, because we can be sure that our cowardice is at that moment being changed into courage.

Shame and guilt are the death of body for the sake of our soul. Courage and humility are operations of soul, which can be effective then as our new mind or our new body. remember that our mind is our soul as visible, while our body is our soul as invisible.

99

We still have one thing to look into, and that is the cowardly emotion which is not any more a disability but has become an inability, in such a way that we wonder what has happened to our energy, with our zest for life, with our spontaneous joy. Gradually our moods are dragging us downwards and we experience despair. Again, when we search for reasons for this despair, or for a cause, we soon find one, or even several, because the despair is willing to produce them for us ad libitum. It is as if we stared down into a bottomless pit and gradually, from sheer dizziness, everything begins to turn and we slide, we sink, we fall, fatally attracted by the thing we most abhor. The myth of the underworld was fabricated to deal with this, and the modern hell beckons and repels there. More recently we have such inventions as 'the unconscious' and 'the subconscious' to console us, if it should happen that nothing better comes our way. Of course it always helps too if we look for something better.

Anyone with true compassion can show us something better. As emotion disappears we are left high and dry. Or, let us say more accurately: As our emotions, our pleasurable, disabling emotions burn out, we are left high and dry, and far from realizing that we are well rid of something that did us no good, we hanker for it back. The compassionate one stands by us and out of companionship supplies what is missing in ourselves, namely passion. Not an example of action is what we need, but an example of passion. Our standpoint is wrong, our point of view is perverse, we hear and see the opposite of reality and we feel nothing but shadows and spectres. Our inward self, to which we give credence, is a yawning abyss, but the compassionate one beside us protects us in a way that we cannot yet fathom. He holds out to us the hand of friendship without demanding that first we should change. He does not say: "Do this, do that, and pull yourself out of this hole," because he knows that precisely what is amiss with us prevents us from doing anything sensible or rational at all. He may have preached at us for a while, but then he realized that we quite simply just cannot help ourselves. Of course he may speak to us, but then his words will be outright compassion and nothing of condemnation or of advice. He recognizes our state and refuses to judge, since he knows that he cannot know how we came into our present predicament; besides, the good he can do for us consists solely in his own reliance on passion and in his extension of it to us, as compassion. He limits himself intentionally to passion. Don't forget that he experiences our despair woefully. We have transmitted it to him unawares and he chooses not to turn away from us as the cause, in him, of this despair, but instead to hold out beside us and to translate this despair into hope. If it should occur to him to base such a hope on something other than the creative human/divine spirit he will fabricate yet another myth for us, to which we will then perhaps cling, like a drowning man to a leaking vessel, and our hope will be temporary. Such myths abound, and they differ only in the degree of popularity they achieve, which explains the need for propaganda and evangelism in those who so desperately adhere to them. The truly compassionate one will not attack those myths. It would not have occurred to him to attack that person's previous disability emotions, in which the afflicted one took pleasure. Now that person takes comfort in a myth, and that comfort has to run its course until disappointment sets in, for it is not a true comfort, but as specious as the disability pleasure was spurious.

100

Whence the true comfort?

We could say that true comfort is myth, not a myth, but that would take too much explaining. Besides we have dealt with this in detail in another work.

What the afflicted one needs, whether she is caught up in some disabling pleasure or attached to a short-lived myth, is an inward dependency of her own, that springs from her own human nature, and not from some story concocted to please her feelings, or from some scheme construed to flatter her emotions, or from some plan devised to satisfy her senses. The true comfort she needs is ready to spring from her own human nature but as yet she looks elsewhere, so the compassionate educator looks for ways of drawing her attention not to her passions, that is to say: not to her emotions, feelings and sensations, but to the same human nature on which he himself depends and which is the same for all of us, whether we like it of not.

How can the educator highlight, for the afflicted pupil, the human nature on which he himself gladly depends?

First of all it depends on whether the pupil is an adult or a child, and this the educator determines, if he should be in doubt, by testing his own adulthood, his own adult being, which would be challenged if the pupil were an adult. In the presence of any such challenge the educator will find it quite natural to relate to his pupil powerfully, so that due to this relation the human nature of the pupil is empowered, and therefore more available as a source of comfort. If no such challenge is forthcoming however, the educator will find it just as natural to relate to his pupil mercifully, so that due to this merciful relation the human nature of his pupil is up-lifted, and therefore more accessible as a source of comfort.

Only if the educator is in any doubt as to whether he is relating to an adult or a child does he first test in himself for that challenge, and then the power or the mercy, which were held up by that doubt, are able freely to low. Otherwise he

160

knows right away to relate powerfully or mercifully, where true comfort is required.

101

Human nature as mercy or power is a comfort to us all. We are going to spend some time now estimating the importance of such comfort during the educative process. We are going to assume, first of all, that those who knew the difference would choose the true comfort, which does not temporarily appease some aspect of ourselves, so that we can relax for a time our disability functions or get on in spite of our inability, but it strengthens you and me.

We have noticed how compassion is our way of extending passion to someone who is caught up in passions, and we have shown how these passions can be emotional, felt and sensational, and how they amount to pleasurable disabilities, towards burn-out, or how they become inabilities, towards break-down. We have also given some indication of what we mean by passion as emotion, feeling and sensation, which are our body of knowledge.

Now one of the most difficult things for a learner, when confronted by a compassionate teacher, is the question of how to cope with his ungainly body. We call it 'his', the learner's, ungainly body, but in actual fact it is no more his than the air which he breathes one moment and the next moment it blows him over a cliff. We call it an ungainly body because it gains him nothing. He has not the use of it and possibly resents that he has no control or mastery of it, though at times he wrongly supposes that such mastery or control might be desirable, so he adopts certain standards of behaviour, performs exercises, practices asceticism, takes various drugs, all in this misguided attempt to teach 'his' body who is boss. But what he calls his body is neither his, nor is it body, but all these passions, all these emotions, feelings and sensations, as disabilities or inabilities, that do after all in themselves testify that no such think as a body as yet is owned, and that his soul cannot in fact yet operate as his body. All the various passions are cries of his soul, of himself, for help.

We cannot even justly differentiate between 'our' soul and ourselves unless we have a body. All our attempts to control, manipulate or influence this so-called body, this 'body' of passions, is of course doomed to failure because we mistake the symptom for the thing.

Now a learner, when confronted by a passionate teacher, has his ungainly body, his symptom-body, drawn to his attention, quite automatically, it cannot be otherwise. He would perhaps prefer to remain deluded, because what he experiences in the presence of this teacher is not at all flattering to is ego. He is uncomfortable. He is also unjust. He is not made uncomfortable or unjust, but it is drawn to his attention that he is neither comfortable nor just. He does not fit in, feels awkward, seems to himself unaccountably ill-suited to the requirements of the moment. This teacher knows, even before he confronts that learner, that such discomfort and injustice is going to be experienced by the learner, and he is ready for it. He keeps in mind that the learner is perhaps accustomed to various standards of being and behaving, and that he usually draws energy and justification of a sort from adherence to those standards. The creative teacher knows nothing of standards for himself, but he is probably not wrong in assuming that the learner in front of him has come into the habit of defining his sense of fitting in, and of belonging, in terms of external and internal standards, so that justice means one thing to the teacher, but quite another to the learner. In the same way does strength mean one thing to the learner but quite another to the teacher. The teacher is aware of this, the learner is not.

As the creative teacher confronts the learner, he quite expects, in that learner, a longing for justice and for comfort. But what does the learner really want? He would like to slip back into his standard hiding place, so as to avoid the exposure he experiences in the teacher's presence. At the same time he would like to learn how to do without those standards, which is why he comes to the teacher in the first place, if he is an adult. As a child he experiences the exposure, the aloneness all the same, though his dependence on laws, standards, ideas and principles is much less complicated, since he has not yet made a commitment.

The injustice is experienced all the same by child and adult and expressed in a great variety of ways, some of which may startle the teacher and take him aback. He tries to be ready for as many eventualities as possible, but he himself always deepens his insight and widens his field of operation. The point is, that what the teacher has on offer is not just then the same as what the learner supposes he needs, so the learner is convicted, in a sense, of an insufficiency, which causes him dismay, and he right away inclines to draw all sorts of conclusions as to how this insufficiency should be remedied, but his conclusions follow the old pattern of standards, ideas and principles. It's the old story of: "If I had not come you would not be convicted of failings, but now that I have come you are not only aware of your errors and shortcomings but you also have the wherewithal to make them good."

So this whole business of the learner's unfortunate reaction, initially, to the creative teacher, must be taken into account by the teacher. It would be quite naïve of the teacher to suppose that he can dispense mercy and strength without first experiencing in himself the learner's weakness and injustice. He must always be a passionate teacher, and not hide behind a veil of self-sufficiency or behind a mask of judgment. He must learn how easily this happens, that the mask is put on and the veil is drawn over. Then he must relearn passion, because passion leaves him open to the learner's actual state and condition, which he must experience if he is going to come up with the remedy, with the true comfort. Nothing of the learner's human nature will be transferred to him if he hides or covers his emotion, feeling and sense. If he as yet has no new body and is not capable of passion he has no business calling himself a teacher.

103

If the learner is not comforted, then he will react unfortunately to the injustice he experiences in the presence of the teacher. He will look for some standard justification and the teacher will get confused.

To the learner it cannot but seem as if he has been torn out of his usual way of doing and going. This is confusing for him. He compares his state now to how he was before. He looks back, and hence the experience of injustice. He realizes that he is being judged but he cannot make sense of it. Not the teacher but the creative spirit working through the teacher judges him, and for this spirit the teacher must remain always responsible. This is a weighty responsibility, for which the teacher is held in awe.

It is as if the teacher were saying: "Not I, but the creative good spirit draws your unjustness to your attention. This spirit appeals to you through me and it does not intend that you should experience injustice but that you should be just, that you should fit into the true plan of reality and participate entirely in the orderly and harmonious purpose of love."

We distinguish, for our own purpose here, between unjust and injustice. If a teacher can make this distinction he can save himself a lot of bother, especially with children and adults who tend to rebel. Those in the know realize it is a comfort that this distinction exists. For the learner can become aware of his maladjustment without being demoralized by the experience.

And for the teacher what matters is that he is able to tell as soon as the learner is experiencing himself as unjust and that he does not have to wait until an injustice is experienced, before administering mercy or power. If he fails to notice the learner's predicament due to the creative spirit's influence he will let things come to a pass where the learner cannot help but defend himself against what he experiences as an injustice, and this is then usually condemned as rebelliousness.

So the teacher pays close attention in himself, as he keeps himself alert for all those telltale signs of the fact that the learner has been 'convicted', because this experience of being 'untaught', as we can also call it when the learner notices the gap between where he is and where he might be in terms of knowledge – this experience is transferred to the teacher as indifference, apathy, sluggishness, and just plain as a lack of care. Right way the teacher will incline to chide the learner for not caring, for precisely not being a learner. However he is wise to ignore that inclination and to realize that the learner has arrived at a kind of halfway mark, and that now is the time for the comfort of mercy or power.

104

We sum it up, then, as carelessness, this behaviour of the learner when he cannot any longer keep up with the behaviour of the teacher. And the teacher behaves carefully. He does everything carefully. The carelessness of the learner grates on his nerves. In the adult learner there is a carelessness of both thought and feeling, almost as if for once there were no barriers to keep mind and body in check. The child learner is careless in everything he touches and moves, in the way he opens and closes doors, in the way he dresses and eats, and above all in his speech. This carelessness of speech is especially onerous to the teacher, who has always made such an effort to speak with distinction.

105

It is a carelessness of behaviour and a carelessness of speech. To the teacher it seems as if the learner were rejecting all order and symmetry. And he must know what this means, when this comes over the learner, otherwise he will simply want to stop the disorder, to impose a semblance of order. Otherwise the teacher will say: "Be careful, for heaven's sake, else you will learn nothing and I cannot teach you anything. First sit still and look obedient. First get some regularity into your movements now, some routine into your existence, and try to get used to things happening after a certain predictable fashion. Otherwise nothing will be imparted." This would be an understandable mistake by the teacher. Behaviour and learning have fallen into two categories, and the teacher quite wrongly supposes, hopefully only for a while, that the one must precede and the other, depending on it, will follow. The learning has become a sort of intake, the teaching an imparting, and the behaviour a kind of discipline, which has to come first. The learner is not whole any more, but divided. His attention is not focussed, but bifocal. Half of it is drawn to the way he sits, walks, speaks, while the other half should concentrate on subject matters.

But subject matter has nothing to do with creative learning, just as sitting, speaking and walking, and various things to do with the hands, are not any more behaviour but masks and schemata, adopted and acted out for a questionable purpose.

No, while the learner is careless and disorderly, there and then the teacher has his opportunity for the pedagogic effect. Naturally the teacher is annoyed, and naturally he is vexed. But this is his own human nature in turmoil, and to it he must address himself. Is he not here, in this situation, precisely so that he can offer his pupils a human natural guideline or two?

He forfeits this opportunity if he condemns the carelessness and the disorder as the cause of his discomfiture. Let him call to mind that this is the opportunity for mercy and power, for comfort and care. Let him remind himself that the carelessness and the disorder in fact mean this opportunity.

Of course if this bad behaviour does not vex him, he is probably on the wrong track to begin with. He may be totally ineffectual. Perhaps he is content to be careless and disorderly in himself, in which case he can certainly not be a creative teacher. If his mind is a muddle, his behaviour will reflect that. The pupil automatically will think in terms of being and functioning as in two separate categories and he will either be unhappy and well-behaved or badly behaved and happy. The happy but unruly pupil is as badly off as the unhappy obedient one. Actually neither the happiness nor the obedience can be genuine. One notices in such pupils a tendency to vacillate from one state to the other. The teacher has not yet come to terms with his own human nature with respect to that pupil. Perhaps he does not even care. And if he does care, and consequently is upset, has he understood the meaning of what is going on and has he begun yet to respond mercifully or powerfully?

106

The nature of such a response is worth looking at. We have discovered that in the case of an adult learner the response will be powerful and to the child it will be merciful, and we know how to cope if doubt sets in as to whether the learner is an adult yet.

The raw materials, so to speak, for the response, are the annoyance, vexation and discomfiture which the teacher experiences in himself. Unless he is a very practiced educator indeed he will not merely be vexed, at the beginning, but he will be vexed at his pupils. He will not be simply annoyed, but annoyed with his pupils. So his first task will be to sepa-

167

rate the discomfiture from any attachment to a presumed cause, such as his pupils. His attitude towards his pupils will do the trick. The principle ingredient of that attitude must be forgiveness. He must care for his pupils and wish them well. This is an actual inward move which involves him in person. It won't do simply to ignore the matter; that is not the answer. Anyone who is more accustomed to chastising than to forgiving will have to learn that chastisement without forgiveness is pedagogically ineffective. So the accent is on forgiveness. And here we come to quite a striking insight into the nature of true forgiveness, namely, that to him who is being forgiven the influence is in fact chastening. Our modern attitude is at fault if we suspect a substantial duality here, because there is none except in seeming, perhaps, if the one who is being forgiven supposes, for some reason, that the experience should somehow admit of a self-indulgence. What goes on technically is that for the teacher the discomfiture is removed from any connection with the pupils as a supposed cause, and for the learner some aspect of his ungainly body is rendered gainly.

So on reflection it would seem a modern caution to insist that chastisement should never be without forgiveness, while the contemporary insight discovers that all true forgiveness chastens.

107

Can the teacher forgive the learner his ungainliness? First it must matter to him. He himself must care. If he does not really care, he will seem to forgive but in truth he is only indifferent. The learner exhibits passions. He exhibits emotions, feelings and sensations, as if that were a way to be and to behave, while the teacher knows fine well it is not. The creative teacher hates this ungainly body, which testifies to years of neglect. He hates it because it reminds him of his own predicament. He hates to be at the mercy of his passions, because at such times he is quite powerless, a ball tossed back and forth by fate. He would much rather speak to the pupil and explain, but that would be in vain, because the pupil has not yet arrived at that point where he can be said to be in the possession of his body. The pupil still supposes he can point at his body, little realizing that all he points at is flesh. This flesh is of course no this either, because he makes no allowances for it as organic perception, as his inspirited organ of perception. If that ever occurs to him, it will be much later, once he begins to trust himself in his environment, as a whole being surrounded by world. <u>Organic perception</u> is our inspired flesh informing us of world in reality. We need to make allowances for it as just such a vehicle of information before the process can actually begin. Once it has begun, we remain perpetually informed, and now we can speak of this flesh as ours. A great deal happens now that periodically surprises us.

A creative teacher is aware of his flesh as organic information. Flesh and spirit are for him not any more at war but one and the same. He knows that flesh is inspired and spirit incarnate he is not any longer a slave to the modern polarity. Organic perception renders him his due.

From organic perception as a kind of point of departure the creative teacher is able to dispense mercy or power in the face of 'ungainly body' experience. Organic perception allows him to rise above the turmoil of passions that assail or assault him, so that he is able to deal with these passions creatively.

The hallmark of organic perception is rest. Spirit and flesh are one, and therefore there is rest. This is the rest that has always been missing but now it shines forth.

108

For the teacher who approaches education as an art this rest can only exist in the form of a vague longing for it – but there, and as that longing, it does exist, though often it gets

169

confused with a mere lack of turmoil, with an absence of strife, as though it were not substantial. The creative teacher tastes this rest. He digests, he embodies it. Organic perception functions restfully.

The one who is capable of such rest does not any longer depend on external or internal stimulus. He is no longer motivated by pleasure or pain. He can easily dispense with all the customary mechanical outlets of his nature. What he cannot do is transfer this rest, or the organic perception implied by it, to anyone else. It is growth-related, and perhaps another word for full maturity. It presents itself in the life of an individual human being as a tremendous turning point, upon which a great deal hinges. A symptom of the misunderstanding of it is that there is nothing left to do, that everything has been accomplished, that one has arrived but there is no welcoming committee.

The teacher who knows himself in the possession of his own restful flesh, who is organically perceptive and not any more at the mercy of his passions or powerless before the passions of others, addresses his pupils from a position of sovereignty and is yet most humbly at their service. It is not necessary for them to know what he undergoes for them and what he suffers on their behalf. He willingly suffers on their behalf their mortifications and immaturities as they happen to reveal them to him by transferring them organically to him. He himself is organically fit, so what he takes on is their burden.

109
Education as an Art

Education as an art falls within the context of creative education. It can be discussed most successfully from the vantage point of creative education and the creative teacher does well to understand it completely.

The pursuit of anything as an art implies spontaneous excellence. This sounds like a contradiction, because we incline to think of excellence as achievement upon much labour – and so it is. But the labour is not expended in the direction of the faculty that is to function excellently.

That excellence pertains to one of our faculties, to something that we do, rather than to our being alone, this has to be appreciated at the start. By our faculties we mean such things as our speech, our vision, our muscular facility and the dexterity of our limbs, our thinking and feeling, and so on. Any number of these may combine in an infinite number of ways, so that whoever practices an art, such as the art of healing for example, expresses his own most singular individuality; true art springs fresh from each new human being. We have a right to demand from it the personality of style.

Where confusion arises is in the department of the training of such faculties. If we, for example, imagine something, as a way of behaving or a set of circumstances, then it may occur to us that this can also be imagined well or not so well. We recognize our imagination as a faculty and we distinguish it from the thing imagined. This is a step we take in a definite direction; imagination does not necessarily imply it. We are pleased to have two things before us now, namely an image and the faculty that gave rise to it. What we do next is crucial. If we view the image as the product of our imagination, which seems legitimate enough, we also feel justified in manipulating our imagination, and we may choose to do this in order to come up with an image of our choice. And here the fatal knot gets tied.

110

It depends on how we view our faculties – our imagination in this case. And of course no one can take an art seriously unless he comes to terms with certain faculties of his, and with their products. Imagination is productive of images, and images are nice to have around, always fresh ones, if possible.

But now comes the crunch. Do I think of my imagination as a tool or as an organic extension of my human nature? And how do I feel about the product? Do I want to be able to mass produce it, for the marketplace, in the interest of popular survival, or do I feel that it ought to grow somehow out of my own human nature, and that it should reveal the secrets of human nature in general?

Am I able to make that distinction? Not everyone can. Not everyone can just yet. Not everyone is willing to make it. Too many questions are thrown up. Once I enjoy a sort of sovereignty over my faculties, am I likely to enjoy giving it up? The intellect, for example, seems to lend itself readily to manipulative abuse, at least in our western culture, but this is largely due to custom, not because of anything to do with the human intellectual faculty as such. It thrills us immensely to be able to stand back from the spirit that moves us and then to dictate our measures and means. Our spirit, which seemed at first happy go lucky, compliant, eager to please, turns into something radically different. It turns into nothing but a mere reflection of ourselves. Actually the thing we manipulate so shabbily is not any more our spirit, our human spirit, at all, but the mere shadow of it. As soon as we enter upon mass production we leave our human nature behind and our human spirit flees from us, and what we have left is something that cannot even be described properly, because it barely exists, and because the evidence it gives of itself is self-defeating. Which does not prevent it from making a big noise, of course. Indeed, the biggest noise is made by the last vestige of the self, apocalyptically.

The tricky problem, then, for anyone who would practice an art resides in this: that human natural faculties must be identified, but then they must be allowed to develop naturally while all those powers of self-assertiveness and all those principles of self-sufficiency that unfailingly crop up then are renounced and denied. We call them powers, forces and principles, but everyone experiences the temptation of them in his own way, and especially there where natural resources would otherwise most plentifully abound. By 'otherwise' I mean: If we stand our ground and insist on natural growth wherever the demon comes along with his conveyor belt and promises us the world.

111

Many faculties can be identified, but the one that interests us first and foremost is the exemplary one. The teacher for whom teaching is an art is very much aware of his pupil's natural capacity for imitation, through all the degrees of consciousness. Consequently he desires to give his pupil something worthwhile to imitate. So he develops in himself this facility for demonstrating in the light of day whatever he would like his pupil to learn. If he would like his pupil to learn a sense of order, he sets himself the task of demonstrating orderliness. He may do this in the way he speaks, in the way he moves, in the way he plans his day. An orderly mind will be crucial for him, because the state of his mind is visible to his pupil. He knows this and takes advantage of it. His wish is therefore to set an example of an orderly mind. He consciously sets that example. In other words, he goes beyond the task of keeping his mind orderly inasmuch as he actually knows that he wishes to set an example of an orderly mind. Gradually he learns how to set that example. It may take several days, even weeks. Perhaps his mind has always been orderly but he never has set an example of it, he has never projected this virtue for others.

But first of all he will, of course, have decided that orderliness is missing in his pupil or pupils. He may observe his pupils and decide they are extremely argumentative, perhaps annoyingly so. Now he must ask himself what it might be that is in short supply. He himself must come up with the response. "If only they were more reflective!" he finally decides. "Yes, that's it. If they were to reflect before and while they spoke, their condition would improve." One thing he is careful not to do now is tell them to reflect. That would be senseless. They are neither machines nor mature human beings. He can, however, take for granted their willingness to imitate. They incline to imitation. So he must practice in himself this virtue of reflection and then he must set the example of it. Those are two different things. Of course he is capable of that virtue, otherwise he would not have decided that it was lacking in his pupils. We can see how important it is that he does not readily take anyone's word or opinion for what his pupils need most at a given time. What he himself decides is needed is also what he himself can supply. And he supplies it in exemplary fashion. He does this intentionally, consciously and in full awareness, and especially at such times as when the vice is most obvious.

I see no reason why we should not speak of virtues and vices here. But we must have an indication of how these terms are to be used. Vices are what stands between the pupil and his human freedom. Virtues are what facilitates the attainment of that freedom. Freedom is considered as an end in itself, not like liberty.

The process begins with the detection of the vice by the teacher. He has a practiced eye for the pupil's predicament. He has no intention of bringing it, as such, to the pupil's attention. He knows that if the pupil is a child he cannot be held responsible for it, and if the pupil is an adult, he could be held responsible for it but this would not be very helpful. What the teacher detects or identifies as vicious in the pupil is entirely the teacher's business. It is revealed to him, so to speak, as privileged information. It is revealed to the teacher for the sole purpose that he should come up in himself with the appropriate corresponding virtue. There is neither judgement nor criticisms or condemnation, but discernment and then – invention. If, for example, the teacher finds it is revealed to him that his pupils are beset by a general moral indifference, he will first of all let this insight work on him until it takes on the status of a fully fledged experience. Since his task is to procure freedom for his pupils, he will naturally make it his chief business initially to discover how these pupils of his are less than free. He does not imagine that they are perfect little beings, 'good' children waiting for the blessings of materialist information. He clearly sees children who try to cope in a morally mixed environment, who are beset and infected by detrimental influences in addition to the beneficial ones, and who cannot yet, since they are not adult, discriminate authentically between the two. For the time being we will limit our attention to pupils who are children.)

The insight, that his pupils suffer from moral indifference, must, then, first become fully experiential for the teacher. He has no trouble identifying moral indifference as a vice; often enough he himself is bothered by it. He now seeks to make a compassionate contact with his pupils in these terms. He gets to know them thoroughly as he identifies, not critically but compassionately, this particular malaise. For the sake of our example we have to simplify, because we want to show how the detection of the vice leads to the demonstration of the virtue. The teacher does not chide the children because of their condition; he does not deal in moral precepts. His goal is that gradually the suitably contemporary moral response to these children should arise and develop in himself, organically. This response is to grow naturally in him. His own major input is patience. He is patient with his pupils, but primarily patient with his own inner development, once again in terms of sense, feeling and emotion. We have learned how to refer to this as his passionate nature. He trusts that it develops at its own optimal rate, and that when the time is ripe he will know about it, and then, and only then, will he be able to come up with virtuous responses, demonstrating the antidote to moral indifference, to which he will not even necessarily give a name, but it is bound to be something like moral care. As he then takes moral care with his pupils he is perfectly aware <u>that</u> he does so, and <u>why</u> he does so. He is, in other words, pedagogically attentive and alert.

He sets an example of moral care. His exemplary faculty is the one he develops most assiduously in any case, since he has chosen to view education as an art. And now that it occurs to him how to take moral care of his pupils he does not so much do this as a father who takes moral care of his son (who would not, in any case, choose to distinguish the moral care from any to her variety) or as a friend who takes moral care of a friend, but he does it in singular fashion, as a teacher, in that he sets examples of moral care. It begins organically as the passionate stimulus in himself for which he waited, and then it radiates out as he demonstrates certain attitudes, relates certain instances and selects opportunities to perform certain actions. Always he says to himself in his own secret inner being something like: "I am doing this in order to show how this sort of thing can be done, how situations like this can be handled, how issues of this given nature can be dealt with. I must leave it up to the pupil to absorb my invention by virtue of hs own innate inclination to imitate. I can almost take it for granted that children cannot help themselves, they must imitate, and my example of virtue is much more in the open, much more consciously in the clear light of day, than the sinister and vicious influences that beset the child and cause his, in this case, moral indifference. On account of this clarity, of this intentional and observed sobriety, but also on account of my passionate solidarity with these pupils, my virtuous example will eventually triumph over these pupils' bad habits. Not that I myself take great pride in my virtue; I am not, in general, a moral paragon. As a human being I do battle on the same front along with other human beings, in the struggle against laziness and overzealousness, against vanity and senseless self-sacrifice, but in my vocation as a teacher I show in perfect humility what it means, for example, to take moral care. Of course I cannot set a persuasive morale example as a teacher if as a person I remain indifferent to morality. If in person I remain indifferent and habitually callous to the welfare of those around me, how can I possibly show conviction of care in the examples I set as a teacher? What happens in that case is that my pupils imitate my hypocrisy. I should really leave off and get a job as a standard teacher, where material information is processed and transferred and the human being as such does not come into it.

So I cannot possibly set an example as a teacher that goes beyond my capacity to live as a person. A standard teacher sets no examples but standards, and he sees no reason why he should live up to these himself, even if living up to standards were worthwhile, since these standards are set by the society that hires him to do his job. He can lead the most dissolute life, as long as he leaves it outside the classroom. He may even pursue definite ideals in the classroom which he then sets aside as he closes the door to go home. Such behaviour is not admirable but perfectly compatible with the performance of a standard job. Personal integrity is no prerequisite for 'doing a good job'. But for me education, teaching, is not a standard job but an art, and a vocation."

112

The delusion that teaching can be even less than an art, that it can be a job, needs to be dispelled. The contact between teacher and pupil is such that the worst excesses of the teacher are unconsciously offloaded on the pupil unless the teacher is aware of some of these fundamental laws of psychology. What a child absorbs from an adult within the sort of performer-audience relationship that usually, though not necessarily, constitutes most teacher-pupil activities in a classroom, is first of all whatever the adult tries to hide. We are more familiar with this when we watch a play on a stage and observe how the nervousness of the actors is suddenly within us, and how we then have to make a magnanimous effort to wish the performers well or else be drawn into their collapsed inwardness. The actors on the stage may be not acting at all but only pretending, putting on an act, forcing a confidence they lack, which can make us feel extremely uncomfortable, because once again the one who sets himself up as wishing to do something for us is hiding his fear of not measuring up to the expectations he has aroused – and immediately that discomfort is transferred to us. The more the actor goes out on an emotional limb, pretending to have what he does not have, the more subtly does the thing he hides have an influence on ourselves.

So the better actor gets his inner act together before he communicates, and then he can in fact communicate. Otherwise he offloads his incapacities and infects his audience with his anxieties. And the good actor actually takes into account the present mood of his contemporary audience and shapes his performance accordingly. One audience would fare better with a more lyrical interpretation of certain passages or scenes, while this might be lost on another audience which inspires him in the direction of a more solemn, or perhaps a more frivolous approach.

So if a teacher approaches his teaching as an art, he must be aware of the foremost devices that go into a performance. Certainly a dramatic performance is not the same as an educational performance, but the element of performance must be countenanced in each. An interesting comparison: The actor sees that audience only once, so gradually he warms to it as he woos it and he gets it gradually on his side, so to speak, assuming that his is a worthwhile side to be on. In the end his performance is applauded because the audience has been led out of its everyday routine sensibilities and has been introduced into a state of exceptional aliveness and vitality. (At least that is how it ought to be. Many a so-called actor is applauded for having pandered to the inhumanity of his audience.) The teacher, by comparison, sees the same audience every day, perhaps for several years, but the state of exceptional vitality is to be achieved all the same, so evidently the teacher must warm to his topic, and woo the interest of it, so that his 'audience' may be led, once again, out of an inhibited or exhibitionist state. The dramatic actor performs the same play to successive audiences, while the teacher performs a new play every day, but to the same audience.

The comparison is valid on every qualitative level of performance. Artistry, or the manipulation of the audience for self-gratification, can only be avoided, by both dramatic actor and teacher, if the inward solidarity with the audience or pupils is sought and built on. The central feature here is implicit trust. Neither performer should wait until he judges his audience to be trustworthy but the trust he holds out to those who depend on him for the time being should be based by him on his own confidence drawn from the fact that he knows what he is doing.

Our human liability to stray almost ensures that we pick up from one another detrimental habits. We might express this as a psychological law by saying: "Your liability to stray and mine automatically amass. If nothing is done to counter this tendency, such liabilities continue to amass, to the point of catastrophe. Whenever we strive to perform something as an art, we assume not only responsibility for excellence achieved, but we equally accept accountability for insolence accrued.

179

There are two ways of going beyond custom and the customary; there is the legitimate and the illegitimate way. There is the subversiveness of the artist. He confronts convention and makes promises he cannot hold. His role is illegitimate. There is the lapsed art-worker, who has held what he promised for a while, but then he lost track and sowed only contempt for the customary, his effect is illegitimate. But the art-worker who achieves excellence goes beyond custom legitimately, neither confronting nor subverting the law but allowing that for which laws, customs and conventions exist in the first place, namely human nature, to manifest itself spontaneously here and there.

113

We have isolated mainly one element here that should be of interest to every teacher for whom teaching is an art, and that is the unavoidable transfer of the teacher's doubts and insecurities to the pupils. The more he tries to pretend that these doubts and insecurities don't exist, the more he tries to hide them from the pupils and from himself, the more they insinuate themselves into the pupils, so that the pupils then manifest, openly, what the teacher is worried about. A creative observer can look at a class of pupils along with their teacher and he can soon make out where the shoe pinches.

And it makes sense that this transfer should happen. We are not beset by doubts so that we get rid of them, but because there exists somewhere, for us, a certainty to take its place. Every art-worker accepts his insecurities, as soon as they arise, as doors into fresh areas of insight and strength. The teacher who is an art-worker must do the same. He presents his material in a fashion that must constantly reflect his inner state, whatever that is. If he had inwardly something to hide, his art-work will show it. If he finds himself hiding something, such as an ignorance, an incapacity or an anxiety about something, then his very first ambition must be to consciously work this out, to transform it, so that it is taken up in his art-work, which is what he presents to his pupils. This so-called art-work of the teacher must be looked at by us in greater depth an detail, and then we have to ask ourselves: What is the essence of art as work? What does the conscious, responsible art-worker try to achieve?

114

The art-work of this teacher is what he presents each day, and from day to day, to the pupil. The curriculum states the when and the what. The teacher's art is concerned with the how. The total impression on the pupils is to be that of an art-work. There is the interior of the classroom, first of all. The individual teacher will wish to give it a certain appearance. She will put her own stamp on it, and as the children grow they will collaborate with her in this. There is no question but that it has to be an orderly place for work and play, but children should never be tempted with an environment too com-plicated for them, too full of materials, devices, etc. so that keeping order becomes problematic. So the order, in degree and nature, obviously has to be suited to the work that goes on.

Next comes the appearance of the teacher. If she dresses in accordance with some standard she will find it hard to live with pupils whose clothes may be shabby. And yet it won't do that her manner is slovenly, or that she 'dresses the way she feels'. So once again, her outward appearance, much like the appearance of the classroom, must be allowed to reflect her individual character. She speaks with her clothes even as she speaks with the interior of the classroom. In these things she must set not the trend, but the pace. She knows what dif-ference appearances can make, and a change of appearances at the crucial time, and she has learned that mere appear-ances, as separate from character or tied to some standard, has nothing to do with art. Always and again character must take possession of appearance and shine through. The school-grounds, the buildings the landscaping, this should be earnestly discussed by the teachers in concert and give evidence of a common effort and attention

115

And then the curriculum. What does the teacher choose to talk about, what does she say? She is going to draw the attention of the children to something. "Look at this," she is going to say, and: "Look to that." The teacher is an adult, so it must be entirely up to her what the topic for discussion is, or what the pupils are going to do. If she is going to teach artfully she must be deciding for herself what it is that will serve her as a hook for her attention. Her artwork is going to consist first of all of attentiveness. She will not say: "Pay attention!" – as if the attentiveness had to come first and then some matter in hand, but she will take some matter in hand and take an active interest in it, herself, almost as if she were seeing it for the first time. So she attends to this matter, and her own attentiveness must eventually involve the attentiveness of the pupils. What is she doing? Is she learning something about the North Coast of Ireland here? She sounds as if she were wondering about it. Has she not spoken several times about the North Coast of Ireland? What, if anything, does she really know about it?

Ah, she hasn't collected an assemblage of facts about it. When she talks about it, she sounds as though she were there. No mere hear-say passes her lips. She seems to know how to approach this matter in a way that involves herself, her thought and passion. One gets the impression that she has not launched herself into a theoretic tirade, nor is she presenting mere dead information, but what she talks about she cares about. How does she manage to sound not at all pedantic? One might almost say she herself is learning at that moment. She keeps the children in mind, she keeps herself in mind – and she keeps the North Coast of Ireland in mind. Also she talks as if she would not at all mind being interrupted, so evidently she is not giving a speech, but speaking. And gradually something is building up. One really has to be there to experience this. She surrounds her topic with a myriad side issues. Some Geology plays into it, some comments on bridge building, on salmon fishing, on the erosion of beeches. A devotee to the academic approach would wonder what the point of it was, because it will not be squeezed into a category. There is no doubt that this teacher herself is frequently surprised by the notions that occur to her, and she finds them delightful. The coast of Scotland is visible from the top floor of the Bushmills Distillery. Puffins sail in and out of the rocky caverns that are lashed by the Atlantic Ocean waves. Tone and mood evidently seem very important. A cheerful sensibility prevails. What is building up is an atmosphere, a quality of perception a sense of adventure. And nothing is forced. This lady is not concerned with losing her audience, nor with losing her thread. One feels perfectly relaxed in her hands. "Imagine yourselves on the North Coast of Ireland" she says, but what she means is: "Imagine!". Imagination is her strength. Art without imagination is inconceivable. Her own is alive and kicking, full of vitality; she never repeats herself. She has what it takes to enter a field of study and to populate it, to realize it. She has imagination. She knows that without imagination she would be lost. But so would her pupils be lost. They expect it from her, though they would not know how to identify it. One last word about Dunseverick Castle, about the Storm Petrel, about a mist of rain that soaks you through in a trice, and the hour is over.

What has happened to those pupils? What has been done for them? Are they better off now than before?

116

Not that this teacher has images ready when she enters the classroom. This cannot be emphasized enough. A familiarity with her topic, gained through diligent preparation, not the night before, but on diverse occasions, this is her chief concern prior to the event of the art-work in the classroom. Should she be able to answer idle questions in detail, and correctly? But that's not the point of the exercise. She leaves it to her imagination, indeed to the spirit of the moment, to select for her the various areas of interest as she builds up her work. Questions will come, and should be allowed to come, especially from a wide-awake group of pupils who are encouraged to participate in this imaginative venture. Memories of related experiences are offered and shared. Where a child takes an interest at variance with the spirit of the venture, this is discerned by the teacher and kindly corrected. False impulses are simply ignored.

But the teacher has nothing in mind, no dogma, into which the spirit of the children must fit. Art is venture and quest. Therefore she guards, in herself, against a vengeful spirit that would quench. This vengeful spirit is known to every worker of art. It stems from an insistence on self, on the selfish path and it sets itself up as a judge or critic. Its effect is destructive, especially so wherever it pretends to be constructive.

This <u>vengeful spirit</u> is judgmental and critical. Get to know it or your art will be cankered at the root. Envy, spite and malignancy stand poised in the proscenium of our heart.

The task of this spirit is to squash every sign of individual originality, sarcastically, embittered or in a rage. The liar is afraid of it and limits himself to the ineffectual niceties of sweetness and light encapsuled as venom.

117

It is this particular vengeful spirit which would keep a class of pupils enthralled and the standard, totally uncreative teacher actually depends on it for control of the class. Not that he would admit this, for in his eyes he merely relies on this spirit to help him 'stay on top of any nonsense'. His definition of 'nonsense' is interesting. Whatever still dares to rebel, in the child, against 'input of info', against 'strain-training', against 'force-feeding', is nonsense, must be given a variety of bad names and expunged. Discipline, authority, order and obedience are all defined in terms of this polarity, with the vengeful spirit on one side and signs of original individuality on the other.

The artful teacher knows this spirit and is ready for it. She actually expects it to rise up in her at any unforeseen moment. It will not be shut out but may be detected immediately. Then begins this teacher's most crucial task. Within her burns a semblance of righteousness and she thirsts for justice. Now she must ask herself how her art is best served. As long as she resists this spirit she aggravates her situation. She must find another, and stronger, spirit to see her through. Every art-worker knows this spirit too and associates it in his mind, after much experience and practice, with his experience of the vengeful spirit, because there, at that intersection, where once again the vengeful spirit is ready to obliterate opposition, the <u>spirit of kindliness</u> stands ready too and waits to be asked.

118

It is a simple case of switching over, from one spirit, that besets and possesses her, to another, that yields itself to her insensibly. The former took possession of her senses, the latter leaves her free to be sensible. What should be simple seems difficult only while she is addicted to the vengeful sensation. And it is, by definition then, an addiction, because she actually tries to achieve something, to bring something about, vengefully, and she gets pleasure from such futile attempts – only at the moment, of course. Afterwards she realizes to her chagrin that once again she has given in to destructive forces and now she has the penalty to pay, in terms of shattered nerves.

Eventually she is bound to ask herself: How can I make myself much more akin to this kindly spirit? What can I do, how can I behave, to make myself much less accessible of this vengeful spirit, especially now that I have acquired, to my shame, a pleasurable attachment to it?

And there, even from her own lips we learn the remedy: "to my shame". She must learn to be ashamed. A repentance is necessary and shame fills the bill here. She may not be able to fathom shame, except as an accidental feeling, to be repressed quickly. But such feelings can give her a lead, to what will turnout to be a conscious and intentional deed within herself.

She will learn to feel shame, and to be ashamed, and in that way she makes of herself a fitting vessel for the kindly spirit, who will then suffuse her entire personality.

119

The notion of the artist as triumphant among men needs to be replaced by the notion of the art-worker as servant. Does an artist know shame? Not as a conscious moral device. But this is how the art-worker applies it. As soon as she notices in herself the vengeful spirit she does not smile and think it a lark because it gives her such a buzz, asserting her self left and right until others are nearly forced to be ashamed on her behalf lest too much damage is done, but she corrects herself shamefully. We have to re-establish this word in its original meaning. A teacher is supposed to have that extra awareness. Where shame comes upon others as an accident, disconcertingly, so that they ask: "What have I done?" and make a mad scramble for justification, for covering up, it is the vengeful spirit that comes upon the one on the artful venture or quest, who then makes herself invulnerable by being ashamed, or by practicing shame – not so that others might change their opinion of her, but so that the kindly spirit will find her acceptable. How can she teach indulging in vengefulness? Again and again we make the mistake of supposing that this vengeful spirit can clear the air for us, that it will forcefully predispose the world in our favour. And of course it is quite true that people are impressed by a show of conclusive force, and that the little devils are momentarily kept in line by a bigger one. But what has a teacher to do with people? Her task is with human beings; the massive appeal is anathema to her. She would rather be overlooked and ignored, while the dust settles.

120

Where teachers try to work in companionship, this vengeful spirit is especially active. Let us imagine a school where several teachers desire to approach teaching as an art. The kindly spirit would have to be prized most highly among them. Let us further imagine that all the teachers of such a school, not just a few, are committed to teaching as an art. What right away moves into the foreground is the contemporary social context of such a school. The school as a whole would encounter, in what we call society, the same problems and tests as every individual person who would practice an art must meet, in this case every teacher. Such a thing as the corporate body of the school must be seen to exist within a social context, just as every art-worker tries to come to terms day by day anew with his personal position, as art-worker, within that same social context. A special difficulty arises because the individual teacher will tend to look to the group for a guarantee of security, forgetting that the group as a whole, entirely on account of the nature of this work, is exposed to the same tests as each member. Everything here depends on insightful attitude. While each teacher practices his teaching as an art and operates with effects and devices that pertain to art, each one according to his own lights, so must the corporation of teachers be seen to operate within the larger social scheme. As the individual teacher's influence on her pupils is to be pedagogic, and since leadership is the essence of that, so almost must the body of teachers as a whole wield such an influence on all those who come into contact with the school, whoever they are. Within the classroom there are the pupils, outside the classroom there are the parents of pupils and the wider community of more or less sympathetic individuals whose support cannot really be taken for granted. Unless this corporate responsibility is recognized and acknowledged, what occurs is something like a society within society, a community within some larger, fancied community, and this is always by definition a seedbed of animosity and strife. At first it seems like a comfort, to relax into a group ethos, where one can let one's hair down and forget about the world. But right away forces come into being that militate against this and dictate that 'this shall not be!' Where two or three get together it must be in the same spirit as inspires each one individually. Where the group is used by the individual as the a launching pad for her own aspirations, creative art is no longer of the essence but policy and cunning. Where an art is to be practiced, the group cannot be used like this, as something to rely on, for effectiveness or security. The counterpart of cunning policy is a cringing slovenliness. Both symptoms could be expected to show simultaneously.

121

We mentioned earlier how the very essence of art dictates that there be progress to creativity, if there is not to be regress to artistry. We indicated that any teacher who wants to approach teaching as an art must resign himself to what happens when he comes up against the common limitations of art, where a crisis sets in.

This growth crisis occurs also in the case of a school where the teachers are art-workers; it cannot be otherwise. Only if such a crisis is recognized for what it means can it be properly seen through an benefitted from.

We may speak of a 'creative impulse', that 'informs' the individual teacher, and also the school, at an unforeseeable time, and when the time is right. Something happens that perplexes and confuses. If the art-worker is not sufficiently experienced, and if the school is not thoroughly enough established, this impulse is misunderstood. Creativity is the essence of it, and it cannot be avoided, but though in itself it amounts to an excellent advantage, if one is not ready for it one cannot help but experience it as negative, inconvenient and destructive. The only thing that is being destroyed is, of course, one's artistry, or the extent to which one has strayed into the bad habit of faithlessly manipulating one's conditions and situation. For the artful teacher there is great need therefore to learn to recognize the symptoms of this destruction and to interpret them correctly. When a school, as an institution, goes into such a growth crisis, those teachers whose art is not grounded 'leave the sinking ship', because all they can see is the destruction. Probably these were the 'artists' on the staff, who cannot bear to be thrown out of their self-appointed roles. Then there are those teachers who sense that something is wrong, but as true art-workers they simply consider this as yet another challenge appropriate to their craft, so they rise to the occasion of the crisis and grow. They become, for a time at least, creative teachers. The school, for a time at least, becomes a creative school, if enough teachers know what is going on and understand it as something that should be welcome, namely as a creative impulse, and not feared, as a destructive force.

And there is such a thing as the corporate reality of that school, that amounts to more than the sum-total of the teachers. This corporate reality of any worthwhile institution is at first like a blessing that rests on it because intentions are sound, but then it must be 'incorporated', which means that it must be taken into account, identified, and given its function.

Actual space must be created for the corporate functioning of that school within its context. If that space is not created and if the function of the school as a corporate body is not acknowledged, it cannot thrive and the institution disintegrates, so that at best one can hope – one has a right to hope – for some sort of a renewal impulse. Some schools totter from affair to affair, and there is never a sound marriage and children. Then those voices are heard, usually, that would guarantee, finally, the standard and standing of the school by financial means, so that "whatever happens to the spirit of the school, at least the bricks and mortar will go on, until the storm is weathered." But such an attitude, such a 'standard' attitude, lies from the beginning outside the consideration of education as art and as creative. From the creative point of view, spirit is inseparable from bricks and mortar, so it makes no sense to speak of sustaining one while the other is absent. Also, from that point of view, it is not the case of an accidental or unfortunate storm to be weathered, but an opportunity for real growth to be taken, as of a crisis to be intelligently interpreted and patiently endured or suffered through.

The standard approach is not compatible with the creative approach. The common denominator is lacking. We in ourselves may vacillate from one to the other, but eventually we must always again decide whether to side with life or with death, with creation or destruction, with organic growth or with stale self-indulgence, and then we draw the consequences.

122

We do well to distinguish between the teacher as artworker and the creative teacher, not because different standards are achieved by them but because what applies for one does not necessarily apply for the other. The art-worker does not envy the creator. The creator does not look down on the art-worker. Both however are aware of their incompatibility with the standard teacher. The standard approach is based upon an entirely different perception of reality and human being.

And the way a school is managed must differ along similar lines. The perception teachers have of their school must be such that no inappropriate methods are used to try to support and perpetuate it. Embalming fluid does wonders for a corpse but impairs a body. Conversely, good bread and wine sustain a body but do nothing for a corpse.

So, when we speak of a creative school we mean something very specific. We mean something that is instituted in a peculiar fashion and supported in a singular fashion. Methods and means of management that would serve marvellously to keep up the appearances of a standard school would actually work detrimentally if applied on behalf of a creative school. We have already mentioned how the financial aspect of creative school management cannot and may not be approached separately from the school's educative function. Either money is a basis or else it is not. Within the creative context money cannot be basic. Therefore it must always be seen as a guideline within which such a school operates. The cry: "If only we had more money we could function so much better!" is relevant for a standard school, but within the creative context it must be condemned as fatuous. Available funds are not potential for growth but productive limitation. They are one of the man productive limitations, along with number of pupils, of teachers, of helpful parents, etc. potential for growth resides in, and springs from, the marriage of human being with creative impulse. When something is sensed to be insufficient or inefficient, both remedy and supply must be sought there, where human being is informed by creative energy. And since the supply of creative energy is infinite, the onus is on human being, and, more to the point, on human beings, and on whether or not we are open and available to this infinite energy, and whether or not we know how to draw from

191

this ever available source of strength – and on whether or not we bother to do it.

A creative impulse would never occur to a standard school. Where we work according to a standard we have made up our mind beforehand as to what shall apply, be suitable, have relevance, so that the future is closed, is a state predicted in line with the past. A creative impulse however must enter into us and into our work presently. And what we do as an art takes account of this. We are willing to be surprised right now. We know that the work we do is informed by a being greater than ourselves, and that we cannot be greater than that being. These two facts are ruled out by the standard approach.

123

Terminology is important. It seems readily acceptable to speak of creative teachers in a creative school, but we know by now how much is involved in this and how much is implied. And the difference between art and creativity needs to be shown. It seems awkward, and not so readily acceptable to speak of an artful teacher, but we need a word to describe what a teacher does who approaches teaching as an art but is not consciously creative. We feel tempted to speak of the teacher as artist, but find it impossible to apply the term artist except in a pejorative sense. This difficulty, I mean the difficulty of knowing what to call a teacher for whom teaching is an art and who is neither fully creative nor artistic, is explained by the situation in which such a teacher finds himself, since he must now and again rise to the level of creativity, and usually after being in the throes of a creativity crisis, having experienced, in one way of another, a creative impulse. So we do well not to label such a teacher in a way that would tempt us to forget his special status.

Neither should such a teacher wish to forget his special status. She should know of creative impulses as actual experiences and she should get herself into the habit of welcoming them. The uncomfortable side-effects should eventually be well-charted territory. When it is high time for a teacher to learn something new, others rally round and the atmosphere is one of tense expectation. Then, too, there is the recurring problem of artistry which has to be faced. But both this risk of artistry and the creativity crisis have special bearing on this teacher as art-worker and they form, as it were, the left and right bank that contain the stream of her passionate activity.

It remains highly significant that the pain such an art-worker either suffers or resists is identifiable conveniently in terms of artistry and creativity crisis, where the artistry is a symptom of that modern ailment called criticism and the creativity crisis is a manifestation of creative impulse. We indulge in criticism when we have not yet come up with enough trust in our inward human security, and the resulting difficulties then cause us dismay so that we step up the criticism. Trust lets us break out of this vicious circle, and every art-worker, teachers too, have to learn to fathom the depth of this practical trust, so that pain can be suffered and not resisted. A creativity crisis, in turn, has a disorienting effect, so that we tend to panic and close ourselves to the influence that would prefer us open. The future looks dark and we are persuaded of our own worthlessness. "There is no hope," we say, and yet we precisely should at that moment hope. Hope, intentionally and consciously practiced, not because we can put our finger on something particular to be hoped for but because we know that hope gets us through a dark patch, is extremely effective during such a creativity crisis, but alas, the practice of it is a lost art. Part of the contemporary art-worker's task, therefore, is to rediscover hope, not hope as a feeling but as a virtue, as something done and persevered with. An art-worker does not need to be reminded that reality supports human life, and that reality exists whether he can just sense it or not. He is in the business, after all, of testifying to reality, for the benefit of those who have lost track of it or who have not yet experienced it as ever present and providential. The teacher as art-worker testifies daily to the reality of human nature and human growth in the face of a great deal of seeming evidence to the contrary. Trust and hope are his two great levers, so that reality as true and beautiful will time and again be given its distinction, where pupils may put themselves against it and base themselves upon it. The teacher's experience of reality is therefore of primary importance and deserves to be moved into the forefront where we try to come to terms with such a thing as teacher training.

An emphasis on experience of reality is crucial where teachers are to be trained. A short discussion of this might be in place here.

The standard educator views reality generally as 'the way things are', and by this he means, philosophically speaking, mere appearances as recorded by individuals and agreed upon for the purpose of survival. The art-worker really begins by saying that reality is not this at all but true and beautiful experience in communication. He arrives at this inwardly and then, upon arrival, recognizes it outwardly.

To the extent that teachers are more or less mature adults, they are capable of inward and outward experience. They are capable of each of these as distinct, though not separable, from the other. However although they are capable of it, they may not be in the habit of doing it. And their proficiency as art-working teachers depends on the ease with which they can draw on distinct inward experience and then refer to distinct outward experience and then combine the two so that there is, so to speak, a marriage of the two, which could then be called the finished art-work of the teacher.

Before we go into particulars, let us be quite aware of what is at stake here. Outward and inward experience cannot be artfully married unless they first exist in distinction. So our

194

first task is to work out this distinction of each. Indistinct experience usually amounts in all of us. We are stimulated in a great variety of ways, pleasant and unpleasant, from outside and from inside, organically, mechanically and just plain accidentally, and all this makes for a confusion of elements which tires and exhausts us as it stresses our various members and causes tension and strife. As art-workers and as creative human beings we are committed to the highly responsible business of ordering this chaos, and as teachers we are even willing to do it for others and to show them how to do it. Our notion of reality is such that we cannot possibly imagine how this chaos of indistinct experience can be real. consequently we set ourselves the real task of always first ordering our own confused minds and bodies, and only then do we take on the confusion of others. And we know by now that the confusion of others is readily transferred to us, and then it becomes ours, and right away our own art-work priority.

Adults can be trained if they are willing to be trained. Basic training towards distinct experience involves a gradual process of identifying experience as inward or outward. This identification is itself an art process, and therefore to be viewed as work, and not as 'life'.

We can describe this process as a gathering. What we gather inwardly has to do with what we think and feel at that moment. Someone who is willing to be trained agrees to stand for a short period of time in front of a few others, one of whom is a trainer, and as he stands within this area designated for the purpose, something akin to a stage in front of an audience, he is requested, for example, to invent a scene that surrounds him. He imagines what he likes, envisions it, and then describes it for the others in such a way that it comes alive for him and so that he feels comfortable with it. This is a start. He may tell his friends, who are at that moment quite removed from him and 'in another world', such as an audience is removed from a drama actor, that: "Behind me extends a long wall, sandstone, higher than myself. I stand with my back against it. To my right ... trees, bushes, a hut, in front of the hut a pile of logs, an axe sticking in one of them. To my left ... several men approach, up a hill, towards me. Straight in front of me ... an incline towards a castle ... no, not a castle, but an unusual structure, mostly glass, round towards the front, black glass ..." He continues until he feels quite content with 'where he is'. The trainer may decide that something is being done excessively and in that case he may put a stop to it and ask: "Tell us in greater detail about the approaching men ... about the wall behind you. Now turn around and face the wall." All is limited, at first, to vision, with the eyes. Limitation is crucial. The trainee agrees to the limitation and endeavours to honour it.

At another session the trainee is asked to touch what he has envisioned. A distinction is made between envisioned and recalled experience, and each is practiced separately. Then one gradually moves into the area of feeling and emotion. Aesthetic distance is always preserved. The trainee steps into a realm of his own, which he furnishes, and he relates what he experiences in this realm to his audience, who themselves have the important task of inwardly supporting the trainee and wishing her well, so that a real atmosphere is created. Only the trainer moves from one realm to the other. The trainer must be a creative person, so that he can, so to speak, oversee the art-training.

The trainer suits his program to the trainees. Since he operates creatively, no program can be laid down for him but he invents and discovers it as the sessions progress. The trainer's creativity facilitates the trainee's art. He himself frequently should demonstrate the art he has in mind by stepping into the aesthetic realm himself and setting examples.

Peace and rest predominate during these sessions. One proceeds reflectively, on the look-out for skills and in search of insight. These skills and insights are all those of the art-worker, who learns how to gather experience here and now. His art, whatever the mode of it, is fundamentally this gathering of experience here and now, not like a tourist or like a mystic, but as a growing human being. (The tourist might be seen to gather outside, not outward, experience, while the mystic gathers inside, not inward, experience. Theirs is less a gathering and more an amassing. Inward and outward experience can only be gained in compassionate relation to others, not in isolation for self-aggrandizement.)

124

During a training session everyone gets several opportunities to practice, so that he can follow up discoveries and relate to the progress made by the others. A most important thing for the trainer to ensure is that the atmosphere is always contemporary. Even if no one else is aware of it, he at last must be in contact with contemporary realty, and he must know how to get back to it, primarily within himself, if he has gone astray. It is not enough for the trainer to be an art-worker; he must be creative. We know by now what this means. He knows how to learn on the spot because his mind is clear of preconceptions and presuppositions. He is able to discern spirits, to discriminate between the genuine and the sham.

125

Outward experience is best envisioned, during training, while inward experience is best enacted.

The trainee is invited to enact his present mood, for example. As he searches for it he moves about within the practice space. Mime is useful. He does not try to entertain the others or to relate something to them. He acts as if they were not there, but he welcomes the tension their presence puts him under. If this tempts him to show off, or if it embarrasses

197

him, there he has some inward experience to come to terms with. He may then describe the mood that has surfaced, such as sorrow, depression, excitement, enthusiasm, etc. Last of all, if ever, will he name them. His central ambition is to become, to enact, to be responsible for – his real contemporary mood. He might limit himself to expressive movement of body, of head, arms and legs, of face and hands, and then, after that practice 'moment', others might wish to comment. What did they see? How were they moved? How does this compare to what the trainee imagines he expressed?

But verbal identification is not of the essence and discussion should be kept to a minimum.

The trainer introduces the individual trainee to various areas of sensation, feeling and emotion that are yet to be discovered. "Be glad, please," he says to a trainee, who then does his best. Another tries. "No, you are pretending," the trainer decides. "Don't try to satisfy us, but yourself. Enact gladness, do not imitate what you suppose would be the behaviour of someone who is glad." Some trainees can readily be courageous but not joyful, others the other way around. The trainees learn from one another empathetically and on account of their will to gather as much experience as possible.

126

Really we can sum up by saying that the trainee teacher is encouraged and helped and guided by the creative trainer to give examples of virtues, as outward and inward experience at first, and then later as a marriage, or union of these. The training is itself an art process, and this is of crucial importance.

By virtues we mean conscious and intentional expressions of our human nature. That which is unconscious or accidental has to be reworked. It is virtuous to both do and know what we do. To be hopeful and to know that we are being hopeful, this is virtuous. More emphatically, it is virtuous to hope and to know that we hope, to feel and to know that we feel, to think and to know that we think.

127

The division of experience into inward and outward is important because so much of our experience is massive. It is amassed, indiscriminately, as though we were puppets of fate and not free human being. And we do indeed more and more become such puppets the more we behave as though we were puppets.

The teacher himself must know what it means to be free. He must know the pleasure, the great pleasure, of being free to do. If he supposes that circumstances, conditions or environment prevent him from freedom he is labouring under a misapprehension, for these cannot prevent him. He has brought it upon himself that it should seem so to him and now he needs to be informed of the true nature and source of freedom, even though he has for some years called himself a teacher. And yet the discovery of the inward mainspring of freedom involves a long and laborious process of learning, and this process we describe at the moment. We show how the trainee may ask himself – at a time and place set aside for the purpose, in the presence of some who wish him well and at the same time removed from them by the use of a barrier which, for the time being, we describe as aesthetic – how he may ask himself: "What exactly is it, this inward realm? Let me make such a thing as my inward experience relevant to these others who observe me at the moment and who crave an example of it." And so, perhaps, he begins: "I am not well adjusted. I feel I am empty here where I should be full. The warmth of familiarity has left me entirely. Perhaps this should alarm me, but even as I describe what to my judgement is really a deplorable state of things and a lamentable situation, this inward realm becomes somehow inhabitable and I thank you for helping to create the opportunity for it."

That might be it the first time. The trainee has done something crucial. He has set an example of willingness. And he has allowed himself to be informed on the spot of certain facts about himself which he then related. He has trusted that his good willingness would suffice to bring him within this inward realm of experience even though at the start he had no evidence whatsoever of such a realm. He has enacted for these others inward experience in the making and he deserves to be thanked for it. The trainer comments on the evident genuine concern of the trainee for the truth of the experience enacted. There was no pretence, but honesty; nothing merely repeated, but fresh communication. Certainly the trainer refrains from criticism. Whatever he dislikes he deals with within himself, since he knows what it means to be creative. He limits himself to a very few positive comments.

128

When we observed, above, that "the trainee allowed himself to be informed ..." we referred to a main theme that runs through all art. Teaching as an art involves it and presupposes a familiarity with it. It is the theme of an inward openness to the truth in one form or another. It is the openness, the receptivity, to true inward experience. What needs to be known in relation to this and what is frequently ignored by us if we are either hasty or lazy is that we will not be inwardly informed unless we are prepared to share this information. Our readiness of speech, for example, must precede if we are to receive something to say. The art-worker shares with us what he knows to be infinitely available to him, but he knows that none of it is accessible, neither to him nor to us, unless he sets out to share freely what he is then given.

If the trainee keeps this in mind while making his first few essays into the realm of inward experience he will much more readily succeed. His task is not to entertain or to confess but to communicate. Communication is really the best word for it. Remember that what he comes up with is useful and good, and that he himself has as much the benefit of it as we do, so he is not merely something like a pipeline or a delivery service.

All this has to do with a proper understanding of what this division of inward experience amounts to. I use the term 'experience' because of the way it happens in general to be used these days. It puts us in mind of what G.M.Hopkins meant by 'inscape', or R.M.Rilke by 'Innenraum'.

129

The second trainee steps into the work area. His brief is still simply to come up with inward experience, for himself and for those who 'have his presence to themselves'. He waits. Even the waiting he does is artful. Pressure, anxiety – he notices. He knows that even as he stands here he is practicing his presence to these others. He might remind himself: "I stand here for them. I have stepped into this beautiful circle for them, so that they might have the benefit of my presence entirely for themselves. My genuine human appearance is an excellent thing for them now. I do not pretend to be here when in fact I am busy in my mind with other things, but my inward being is entirely demonstrated at this moment. Now I will move. Now I will speak." The 'audience' occurs to him as an inward challenge. Their expectations are turned by him into personal responsibility. This is important for the teacher, whose audience is often, if not every day, the same. He wishes to become eminently responsive to the way that his pupils are today, just now.

Really what he must begin to fathom is how beauty operates. Art and beauty are inseparable. He must know that he sets out to take advantage of this operation of beauty by choosing to step out and in front of 'these others'. This act is a fully responsible one for him; he has no intention to work magic, to mystify or to astonish. He does not wish to take

201

advantage of the effects of beauty to serve his own ends, but he knows that beauty, if given half a chance, works miracles. He has been told as much, he has observed it, and now he is to mediate between beauty and his 'audience'. If he behaves in a certain way, beauty shines forth.

130

What is this behaviour? It definitely pertains to inward experience. It presupposes in us an awareness of our inward being, and then an awareness of it as whole. The trainee can say: "I am whole and I inwardly know it. This knowledge is precious to me and I wish to extend it to others. But this I can do effectively only while I relinquish all personal possession of anything to do with this inward experience of being whole. This personal possessiveness is a dangerous trait and I must do my best not to fall foul of it. How do I manage that? By always and again insisting that beauty be personal. My inward experience of being whole must be personal, and again personal, and this takes training because my tendency is ever to make out of beauty a thing. This tendency must be physically, in mind and body, counteracted. If beauty is to function true to its nature and if my inward experience of being whole is to become communication and not run aground as personal possessiveness I may not make a thing of it, as though it might exist in me or for me alone, with no will of its own."

In beauty a will is portrayed that is other than mine and it will not be commanded or controlled by me. This is a difficult lesson to learn. Eventually we learn that this will is merciful throughout, but first we must allow that it is no extension of our own will. Our appropriate attitude in the face of it therefore is – reverence.

131

Now reverence before beauty is perhaps a lost art in our age, so by asking, from teachers, they should come up with such reverence we are almost demanding from them they should step out of the age and become sublime. Is that too much to ask?

At any rate, we will make an attempt to piece together the few scraps of reverence we still hold in our possession. perhaps we can come up with a reasonable facsimile. Beauty is as strong and as glorious as ever but we cannot sustain it and we switch over to charisma at the drop of a hat. You might say that we become attached to the wrong sort of beauty, because the right sort does not allow for an attachment.

But reverence is a disposition of our soul and of our spirit. We generally arrive at it as soon as we notice the risk of an attachment to the wrong sort of beauty. I say we arrive at it, but only if we wish to arrive at it because we recognize the risk. Attachment to the wrong sort of beauty debilitates. Our abilities are destroyed. We ourselves are eventually rendered impotent. So we have to be careful. If we do want real power, which is the ability to do good of one sort or another, we have to practice this reverence in order to come away from this charismatic attachment and so as to be able to stay clear of it.

The practice of reverence is therefore a crucial exercise for anyone who wishes to teach, if his teaching is to be an art. The 'position' of our soul originally, or at any given moment, is such that we value the fruits of perception but we do not perceive. We know what it means to understand and we desire to be understood but we do not understand. This is how usually, and in the beginning, our soul is set. This is not a disposition, but a state. The state of it is as we find it when we come upon it. Even right now, if you were to address your soul, you would come upon it in that state: wishing and hoping to be understood but not understanding. In recognition of this fundamental state of human affairs the teaching is offered: "Do unto others as you would that they do unto you." This teaching commands the basic disposition of reverence.

And whatever else arises out of this teaching presupposes that disposition, otherwise a wrong attachment is involved.

Now as soon as our soul, in its idle state (not passive, but idle) comes into the presence of what we shall call here the light, or as soon as the light approaches it – either of these – it is quite human naturally affected by that light. There is no effect, but an affection. The question to ask now is: How do we respond? Do we, first of all, notice what has happened? We might have striven towards the light, towards clarity and understanding, but now that suddenly we have what we wanted we may be shocked. We may misunderstand. We looked for clarity but we imagined it otherwise. So out of our own misconception of 'that which caused this shock' we tend to produce all sorts of premature entities to which we then become attached. What was missing was our disposition of our soul, so that we might in fact perceive clearly and understand fully.

This disposition can be compared to what we do when first we see the sun, and then we stare at the sun momentarily and are blinded, but then we look upon the earth which is lit up by the sun. We appreciate the sun properly not by studying it but by taking an interest in what it illuminates.

132

Reverence is also a disposition of our spirit. We appreciate how our human spirit moves towards whatever it finds attractive, which is usually that which is most akin to it among all that is available to it. However the personal light is greater than our spirit, and so, while there is attraction, there is also fear. This fear shows up in a variety of ways, as unwillingness, tiredness, even anger and rebellion, and these once again, like the shock in the case of our soul, are to urge us towards a disposition, in this case of our spirit, so that we follow up the attraction in spite of the fear and revere, or honour, the apparent cause of it.

Whether of our soul or of our spirit, this disposition involves a loving in spite of dislike. Resignation and relinquishment play into it.

133

For some who would practice an art, truth is in the forefront. For others it is beauty. There is no need to choose between them. However there is a need to choose. Our communication of inward experience is definite, not haphazard. So if we mistake beauty and the truth for mere extensions of ourselves and for things, for things we can manipulate and control, then we soon run out of inward experience and settle for standards.

However the notion of beauty and the truth as personal rather than as things is not a popular one. We will not be lauded in the market-place for entertaining it, whereas standard notions of beauty and truth are in fact geared and tailored precisely for the market-place. So we have to decide. If we want to buy and sell ourselves we should stay away from education as an art. If, however, we want to be free from all that in order to have life, we do well to consider this notion of beauty and the truth as personal, as something that flourishes on account of its communication, by way of sharing and exchange. If we maintain that beauty and the truth have a will of their own we are often privileged to observe how much succeeds at times simply due to the fact that we have moved out of the way at the crucial moment, that we have effaced ourselves, become anonymous, like someone who has built a road for a prince and then steps aside to allow him to travel on it. How marvellously we are included in the results to that prince's action! We have abundant reward.

134

Beauty and the truth as personal has nothing to do with any imaginations of these in one form or another. We must strictly adhere to inward experience being outwardly expressed for another or for others.

The trainee steps into the realm designated for communication. The others silently wish him well as he searches in himself for experience at that moment. He knows he is being informed and he seeks an appropriate means of communication. It will not be a dramatic medium, since his art is not dramatic acting. His art is teaching. So his medium of expression and communication is the example. He has ample supply, he knows that, in good faith. It exists potentially. If he cannot yet access this supply, this is because he has not yet discovered that particular mode of transmission that is appropriate to the moment. His training is about this, about coming up with the appropriate mode of expression and means of communication. He may choose words. He may have a blackboard behind him, to which he suddenly turns, to sketch on it how he is at that moment, how he would like to be. The trainer prompts him: "You are embarrassed. Include that readily in your message to us. Your embarrassment is experience which you have not yet gathered in, hence it hinders you. Let it become a part of your work, make it an aspect of your example."

The trainee momentarily feels like weeping. She recognizes this as more material and takes it on board, feels it thoroughly, makes no direct reference to it. She then decides, during the remaining six minutes the trainer has allotted her, to relate a childhood experience as truthfully as she can. Not so much the standard truth concerns her, which is something like accuracy of appearances, but the personal truth, which arises out of her present memory for the benefit of her – 'audience'?

"I had left my toys at the foot of the bed. I had many toys, but most of them were broken. My younger brother entered the room and showed me what he had built, strips of metal bolted together, it looked like an aeroplane. I know I should have praised him for it; perhaps I was envious." Her words come slowly, deliberately. There are long pauses between the sentences. She restrains herself from the confession she would like to make, from the entertainment she feels tempted to provide. Then she simply demonstrates: "This is how I walked out of the room. Can you tell how I felt?" she walks back and forth in her allotted space. "This is how I walked. This is the truth of how I was then. I remember it well. Yes, I refuse now to try to recall accurately how I felt. The example I set here is much more convenient, because it suits me right now." She draws a large, easy circle on the blackboard. The trainer stops her. She joins the others. The trainer makes a few comments on exemplary action, on how it gives us a taste of freedom.

135

Have we the will to do all this? Time and again the centre collapses. We do not succeed in what we set out to achieve and we wonder, is it worth it? If art were based on our will, on our insistence and persistence within the confines of self-laid plans, it would be a sorry affair. And this goes for teaching as an art. If ever we knew ahead of time the total end of our endeavours we would lie down under the strain.

But a great part of all art involves the procedure of trial and error. Creation is not like this. While we create we unify from the start our own will with that of our own creator, so that all participates in one. Art, by comparison, is venture and quest. The knight errant rides alongside the knight virtuous and both are accompanied by the knight experimental. All too often it seems to happen that the same path leads this time to quite another goal, or the same goal as last time must be gained by quite a different path. Otherwise two things might happen. We might slip into dead routine or else become irresponsible adventurers. So we need to be inhibited by frustration and spurred on by excitement.

And where art begins to merge into creativity, there we take account of this need in us. We are able to rise above our frustrations and to sink below our excitements ("those twin impostors, victory and defeat", as a poet put it,) not so much because we have accumulated superior willpower but precisely because we have begun to acknowledge our human nature and the potential superabundance of it all. That wonderful invention, our individual will, has lost some of its splendour but something else, something much more important, has appreciably gained.

And that is our willingness to be influenced by love. To our shame we discover how habitually we assert ourselves in opposition to this influence. We do know a love that is allied to willpower and to self-assertion, to insistence on right and to possessiveness, but this love now pales into insignificance before something quite different, something that would move into us and take possession of us and develop in us the organs for the appreciation of it.

This is the love that requires of us that we learn how to suffer.

But even along with the first glimpse we are vouchsafed of this most peculiar requirement we receive a taste of the complete joy with which the texture and fabric of this suffering is shot through. We learn to suffer even as we acquire a taste for complete joy. We must admit that just as suffering as a creative ability would have struck us as an absurdity in the past, so complete joy always and again eluded our grasp, in spite of inordinate exertions of willpower.

We are faced now with the task of rethinking a great number of our habitual motivations and intentions. Actions we performed for one reason or another are bound to seem obsolete. We lay them aside, if only for a time. Justifications we employed to make various indulgences appear reasonable refuse to hold water and are thrown on the scrap heap. Ideals we served reveal themselves as preposterously unlifelike.

136

This ability to suffer becomes then for the teacher indispensible. She does not begin by suffering on behalf of her pupils but something else, something larger, something all-embracive is taken account of by her, and that is the steady and permanent influence on her of the explicitly divine, or of providence. She may have rejected such a notion in the past and perhaps it was presented to her as empty form, but now it stands before her in freshness and power. She senses it distinctly as something formidable and new. In line with our present trend of thought we might say that she moves from art into creation.

She becomes sensible to her contemporary condition and situation in a new way. The change is bound to be painful to some degree, but always and again she will discover how she can adjust to the change.

137

The teacher who allows himself to be led by love will be able to lead pupils. And yet this word 'love' is so empty today that we do well to circumscribe what we mean. It makes no sense to say that we love if we do not welcome hateful impulses, whether they come from within or from without us. Love welcomes hate and so destroys it. Teachers are often hated by their pupils, the pupil would like to be left to himself but the teacher is there to draw him out of himself. There is a conflict of interest. Surely it makes sense that this should be intelligently acknowledged. It we wait until our pupils take a shine to us we will probably hate them back. Who knows but then we may call that authority, even absolute authority. There is such a subtle hate that wears even the mask of love, and for this we do well to watch out. A disingenuous spirit enters and promises to make life easy for us, if only we pretend to be on the side of our pupils. But there should be no side. Therein lies the subtlety.

* * * * *

www.ingramcontent.com/pod-product-compliance
Lightning Source LLC
Chambersburg PA
CBHW060459290526
45791CB00001B/192